WRITE BETTER ESSAYS

IN 20 MINUTES
A DAY

3rd Edition

LEARNINGEXPRESS ®

NEW YORK

Library of Congress Cataloging-in-Publication Data
Write better essays in just 20 minutes a day—3rd ed.
    p. cm.
  Rev. ed. of: Write better essays in just 20 minutes a day
  ISBN 978-57685-792-2
  1. English language—Rhetoric—Problems, exercises, etc. 2. Essays—Authorship—
Problems, exercises, etc. 3. Report writing—Problems, exercises, etc. I. LearningExpress (Organization) II.
Write better essays in just twenty minutes a day.
PE1471.C47 2012
808.4—dc23

                                                                        2011034389

Printed in the United States of America

9 8 7 6 5 4 3 2 1

Third Edition

For information or to place an order, contact LearningExpress at:
 2 Rector Street
 26th Floor
 New York, NY 10006

Or visit us at:
 www.learnatest.com

CONTENTS

CONTENTS

INTRODUCTION ▶

You probably can't even count how many essays you've written for your high school classes. There are essays assigned in English and composition classes, history and civics classes, and language classes. Many electives even require essays. If you're a junior or senior, you know that the stakes for essay writing keep getting higher: they are a part of high-stakes tests like the ACT, Regents', and SAT, and they're required on college applications.

How can you improve your essay-writing skills, not only to get better grades, but also to score higher on tests and boost your chances for admission to the college you'd like to attend? This book offers a step-by-step plan that can be completed in just a few weeks.

How to Use This Book

There are 19 lessons in this book, each of which should take you about 20 minutes to complete. If you read five chapters a week and complete the practice exercises carefully, you should become a more powerful and effective essay writer in one month.

Although each lesson is designed to be an effective skill builder on its own, it is important that you proceed through the book in order, from Lesson 1 through Lesson 19. The material in Section 2 references and builds on what you'll learn in Section 1, as Sections 3 and 4 reference and build on Sections 1 and 2. Writing is a process—a series of skills, strategies, and approaches that writers use to create effective essays. Once you understand the writing process, you can adapt it to your unique working style and to each specific writing situation you encounter.

The first section of the book, *Planning the Essay*, covers the basic prewriting steps that are essential to effective writing. *Drafting the Essay*, Section 2, shows you how to take your ideas and formulate a solid working draft. In the third section, *Revising, Editing, and Proofreading the Essay*, you'll learn how to shape your draft into a clear, effective essay. *Taking an Essay Exam*, the fourth section, provides strategies for writing under the pressure of a ticking clock, whether for an in-class exam or a test such as the ACT or SAT.

Each lesson includes several practice exercises that allow you to work on the skills presented in that lesson. The exercises aren't simply matching or multiple-choice questions. Instead, you'll practice what you've learned by doing your own writing. These practice exercises are central to your success with this book. No matter now many examples you see, you really won't benefit fully from the lessons *unless you complete the exercises.* Remember to keep your practice answers as you work through the book—some lessons will ask you to further develop ideas generated in earlier practice exercises.

To help you stay on track, use the sample answers and explanations for the practice exercises at the back of the book. Check them at the end of each lesson, reading the explanations carefully as you review your response to the exercise. Keep in mind that there is no single correct answer to most exercises. What you'll find instead are *suggested* answers that contain all the elements called for in the exercise.

You'll also find practical skill-building ideas at the end of each lesson—simple thinking or writing tasks you can do to sharpen the skills you learned in that lesson. Some of these exercises ask you to read an essay and examine it for a specific element or detail. You can find essays in many places, such as an English or composition class textbook, or on the Internet. If you have trouble finding appropriate writing, check the list of suggested reading in the Additional Resources section at the end of the book.

To gauge your progress, we'll begin with a writing pretest. You should take the test before you start Lesson 1. Then, after you've finished Lesson 19, take the posttest. The tests are different but comparable, so you'll be able to see just how much your understanding of the writing process and your writing skills have improved.

Different Types of Essays

What makes writing both interesting and challenging is that every writing task is unique. Writing is communication: You are expressing ideas about a *subject* to an *audience* for a *purpose*. Each time you sit down to write, one or more of these three elements will be different, creating a unique writing situation.

Essays are one of many different forms, or genres, of writing. While there are many different kinds of essays, general writing skills and strategies apply to all of them. This book will teach you those skills and strategies, and help you practice them. Specifically, we'll help you apply those skills and strategies to three essay types:

- The college application essay
- Essays for high school and college classes (timed and untimed)
- Standardized, timed essay exams (such as ACT, GED, Regents', SAT)

Section 4 of this book extensively covers the standardized, timed essay exams. Here is more information about how to approach and successfully complete application and class assignment essays.

The College Application Essay

Most colleges and universities require students to submit a written essay with their application. The more than 400 schools that use the Common Application (www.commonapp.org) present five topics from which you must select and write on one. Other schools use similar types of topics, or even ask you to come up with your own.

No matter the topic, the purpose of this essay remains the same: to reveal something personal about you that will give the admissions department a better idea of who you are and why they should accept you. This isn't the time to wow your reader with your insights into current social problems or the poetry of the seventeenth century. Your audience, an admissions officer, want to learn about *you*. A successful college application essay transforms you from a number into a dynamic, three-dimensional person. In most cases, the more real you are to the admissions officer, the more likely it is that he or she will accept you.

Of course, the application essay also gives the reader a sense of how well you can communicate in writing, and that ability is crucial to your academic success. After all, admissions officers are not only looking to see if you're a good fit for the university—they also want to see that you'll be able to handle their curriculum and that you can read and write effectively at the college level.

Here are some Common Application topics and writing requirements found on most other applications:

1. *Evaluate a significant experience, achievement, risk you have taken, or ethical dilemma you have faced, and its impact on you.*
2. *Discuss some issue of personal, local, national, or international concern and its importance to you.*
3. *Indicate a person who has had a significant influence on you and describe that influence.*
4. *Describe a character in fiction, an historical figure, or a creative work (as in art, music, science, etc.) that has had an influence on you.*
5. *A range of academic interests, personal perspectives, and life experiences adds much to the educational mix. Given your personal background, describe an experience that illustrates what you would bring to the diversity in a college community, or an encounter that demonstrated the importance of diversity to you.*
6. *Write about a topic of your choice.*
7. *Submit a writing sample.*

"Write about a topic of your choice" and "submit a writing sample" allow you to recycle something you've written for a class, or even another application (just be sure to change or delete any references to another school).

No matter which topic you select, remember that it is a vehicle for revealing something about *you*, not the historical figure, issue of international importance, or person who has influenced you. But being personal can be tricky. *Anything* and *everything* in your life or about your personality is not appropriate admissions-essay material. College admissions officers note that the worst essays are depressing and/or paint an unflattering picture of the applicant. Think of it this way: Your job in the essay is to persuade the reader to see how you would add to the institution's academic, social, and cultural communities. Your goal is to sound competent, purposeful, and responsible.

Here are some specific strategies to help you write a winning college application essay:

- **Avoid clichés.** The typical admissions officer reads hundreds of essays. It will be difficult to stand out if you write about a subject also chosen by dozens of other students. What has been done too many times before? Here are a few subjects virtually guaranteed to bore your audience: how you've been influenced by a famous person, the death of a grandparent, losing the big game, why you want peace in the Middle East, etc.

- **Narrow your focus.** Most college application essays are 400 to 750 words in length—not enough room to discuss big topics, like your response to 9/11 or your plan to solve global warming with any kind of depth. Think small and personal: what specific experiences or ideas define you as a person? Explore a symbol and/or key moment that best captures you.

- **Avoid hyperbole.** Many applicants make the mistake of trying too hard to win over admissions officers, resulting in outlandish statements that depress more than they impress. Colleges are looking for students who are reflective and resilient; egotistical statements like "because of my leadership skills, we won" or "it changed my life forever" will not impress. Focus on what you have gained from your experiences, and how they inform who you are—and will be—as a student and citizen.

- **Remember your audience.** What you don't know about the reader is important. You don't know if your essay will be read by a 20-something or a 70-something, democrat or republican, male or female, or Christian or Buddhist. You should be mindful of how your topic may be perceived by others. However, you do know that the reader is looking to understand more about you, and only has a few minutes to do so—focus on YOU rather than touchy or potentially offensive subjects.

Essays for High School and College Classes

In almost every high school or college class, you can expect at least part, if not all, of your evaluation for the term to be based on your written work. In a college literature class, for example, most of your grade will probably be based on two out-of-class essays, an in-class midterm, and a final essay, which may be a timed exam. In a political science class, your midterm and final exams might include multiple-choice, short answer, and essay questions. Your success in school depends heavily on your ability to write effectively, both in and out of the classroom.

Types of Essay Assignments

Essay assignments in high school and college classes will be as varied as the instructors who teach them. Most assignments, however, will fall into one of two categories:

1. **The Personal Essay**

   In composition classes and in college placement exams, you will often be asked to write an essay based on a personal experience or observation. Here are two examples:

   Alison Lurie wrote, "Long before I am near enough to talk to you in the street or at a party, you announce your personality and opinions to me through what you are wearing. By the time we meet and converse, we have already spoken to each other in an older and more universal language: the language of clothing." Write an essay in which you agree or disagree with this statement. Use evidence from your personal experience, observations, or reading to support your position.

Here are some strategies for successful high school and college essays:

- **Fulfill the assignment.** Have a clear thesis that directly responds to the assignment, and develop it as required.
- **Provide solid support.** Whether you're writing a personal essay or an analysis essay, you need to show readers that your thesis is valid. Support your ideas with specific examples, evidence, and details.
- **Address complexity.** The most effective essays consider multiple perspectives; if applicable, discuss the historical context and future implications of the topic. In addition, try to draw connections between the topic, the writer, and the real world.
- **Write with clarity and style.** Make sure your sentences are clear and free of errors in grammar and mechanics. Choose interesting words that state exactly what you mean, including vivid verbs and specific adjectives and adverbs.

Describe a time when you presented yourself as believing in something you really did not believe in. Why did you present yourself that way? What were the consequences, if any, of this misrepresentation? How would you present yourself in a similar situation today? Explain.

2. The Analysis Essay

In most other classes, essay assignments will often ask you to analyze specific texts, ideas, events, or issues. Here are three examples from different disciplines:

From a religious point of view, what is truth? Use examples from two different religions to support your answer.

Analyze a local television news program. What stories and events get coverage? How are these stories and events covered? What values and beliefs about America, about the world, and about television and its viewers do you think the news program's coverage reflects?

What illusions does Renoir's film La Grande Illusion *refer to? Discuss those illusions and how the historic events that led to World War I helped foster them.*

3. The Persuasive Essay

In high school, you have probably been asked many times already to address a third category of writing assignment—the persuasive essay. While it is true that most high schools ask their students to write separate personal, analytical, and persuasive essays, in college nearly all essay assignments, whether personal or analytical, are persuasive, or argumentative, in nature. Notice the examples presented to you in this section: in the example for a personal essay, you are asked to agree or disagree with the provided statement; for the analysis essay, the first sample prompt asks you to define truth from a religious point of view, an answer likely to generate many possible responses (hence the need to use examples from two different religions to support your answer). Regardless of the topic or category of the essay, effective writers are always trying to develop and defend their beliefs—everything is an argument!

PRETEST ▶

Before you begin this book, it's a good idea to find out how much you already know and how much you need to learn about the essay-writing process. This test is designed to help you do that. It consists of two parts. Part 1 contains 20 multiple-choice questions addressing several key components in this book. Part 2 asks you to write your own essay and evaluate it according to the criteria provided.

You can use the space on the pages following Part 2 to record your answers and write your essay. Or, if you prefer, simply circle the answers directly for Part 1. Obviously, if this book doesn't belong to you, use separate sheets of lined paper to write your responses.

Take as much time as you need for Part 1 (although 20 minutes is an average completion time). When you're finished, check your answers against the answer key at the end of this book. Each answer tells you which lesson deals with the concept addressed in that question. Set aside another 30 minutes to complete Part 2.

1.	ⓐ	ⓑ		
2.	ⓐ	ⓑ	ⓒ	ⓓ
3.	ⓐ	ⓑ	ⓒ	ⓓ
4.	ⓐ	ⓑ	ⓒ	ⓓ
5.	ⓐ	ⓑ	ⓒ	ⓓ
6.	ⓐ	ⓑ	ⓒ	ⓓ
7.	ⓐ	ⓑ	ⓒ	ⓓ

8.	ⓐ	ⓑ	ⓒ	ⓓ
9.	ⓐ	ⓑ	ⓒ	ⓓ
10.	ⓐ	ⓑ	ⓒ	ⓓ
11.	ⓐ	ⓑ	ⓒ	ⓓ
12.	ⓐ	ⓑ	ⓒ	ⓓ
13.	ⓐ	ⓑ	ⓒ	ⓓ
14.	ⓐ	ⓑ	ⓒ	ⓓ

15.	ⓐ	ⓑ	ⓒ	ⓓ
16.	ⓐ	ⓑ		
17.	ⓐ	ⓑ	ⓒ	ⓓ
18.	ⓐ	ⓑ		
19.	ⓐ	ⓑ	ⓒ	ⓓ
20.	ⓐ	ⓑ	ⓒ	ⓓ

Part 1

1. All essays should be about five or six paragraphs long.
   a. true
   b. false

2. The best place in an essay for the thesis statement is generally
   a. the first sentence in an essay.
   b. the last sentence in an essay.
   c. the end of the introduction.
   d. in the third paragraph.

3. A good introduction should do which of the following?
   a. grab the reader's attention
   b. state the thesis
   c. provide the main supporting ideas for the thesis
   d. both **a** and **b**
   e. all of the above

4. Your relationship with your readers has an effect on how you write your essay.
   a. true
   b. false

5. Which of the following best describes the problem with the following paragraph?
   Sullivan studied 25 city playgrounds. He found several serious problems. The playgrounds were dirty. They were also overcrowded. They were also dangerous. Many parks had broken glass everywhere. Many parks also had broken equipment.
   a. lack of variety in sentence structure
   b. grammatical errors
   c. lack of transitions
   d. poor word choice

6. Which organizational strategy does the paragraph in question 5 use?
   a. compare and contrast
   b. chronology
   c. problem → solution
   d. order of importance

7. Read the following essay assignment carefully. Determine which answer choice best describes the kind of essay you should write.

Some say ignorance is bliss. Others claim that ignorance is a form of slavery and that only knowledge can set you free. With which view do you agree? Explain your answer.

   a. explain the difference between ignorance and knowledge.

   b. explain which belief you concur with and why.

   c. explain how you think we can improve education.

   d. discuss the evils of slavery.

8. Which of the following organizational patterns applies to all essays?

   a. order of importance

   b. cause and effect

   c. assertion → support

   d. problem → solution

9. A *thesis* is best defined as

   a. the prompt for an essay.

   b. the main idea of an essay.

   c. an essay that is at least three pages long.

   d. the way a writer introduces an essay.

10. In the following paragraph, the first sentence is best described as which of the following?

More and more Americans are turning to alternative medicine. The ancient art of aromatherapy has gained a tremendous following, particularly on the West Coast. Acupuncture, the traditional Chinese art of needle therapy, has doubled its number of active practitioners in the past decade. And holistic medicine—treating the whole body instead of just one part—is so popular that some HMOs now even pay for holistic care.

   a. a transition sentence

   b. a topic sentence

   c. a supporting idea

   d. a thesis

11. In the paragraph in question 10, the second sentence is best described as which of the following?

   a. a transition sentence

   b. a topic sentence

   c. a supporting idea

   d. a thesis

12. Which of the following should a conclusion NOT do?

   a. bring in a new idea

   b. restate the thesis in fresh words

   c. provide a sense of closure

   d. focus on the reader's emotions

13. Words and phrases like *meanwhile, on the other hand*, and *for example* are known as
   a. passive words.
   b. assertions.
   c. modifiers.
   d. transitions.

14. Which of the following strategies is particularly useful during an essay exam?
   a. brainstorming
   b. freewriting
   c. outlining
   d. journaling

15. Brainstorming typically takes place during which step in the writing process?
   a. planning
   b. drafting
   c. proofreading
   d. revising

16. *Revising* and *proofreading* are interchangeable terms.
   a. true
   b. false

17. Support for a thesis can come in which of the following forms?
   a. specific examples
   b. expert opinion
   c. anecdotes
   d. both **a** and **b**
   e. **a**, **b**, and **c**

18. Never use a one-sentence paragraph.
   a. true
   b. false

19. What is the main problem with the following sentence?
   Newman lost the election because of the fact that the opponent whom he ran against had a lot more money for ads.
   a. It's a run-on sentence.
   b. It's not properly punctuated.
   c. It's unnecessarily wordy.
   d. It lacks parallel structure.
   e. There is no problem with this sentence.

20. Which of the following strategies will make an essay more convincing?
   a. avoiding run-on sentences
   b. acknowledging counterarguments
   c. providing specific examples and details
   d. both **b** and **c**
   e. both **a** and **c**

Part 2

Set a timer for 30 minutes. When you're ready to begin, carefully read the following essay assignment. Use the space provided to write your essay. Stop writing when 20 minutes have elapsed, even if you haven't completed your essay. When you're finished, look at the scoring chart in the answer key to estimate your essay's score.

Essay Assignment
Many people have been profoundly affected by great works of art. Describe a work of art—a book, a movie, a photograph, a drawing, a painting, a song, or a musical composition—that had a powerful impact on your life. What work of art was it? How did it affect you? Why?

1 ▶ PLANNING THE ESSAY

While creativity and inspiration can play an important role in good essay writing, planning, drafting, and revision are critical. Whether you have to write an essay in class, during a test, or at home, getting down to the business of writing means focusing on these three things. They benefit your reader by showing him or her how the various points you make in your essay work together and how they support your thesis.

When you begin your essay with planning, you will have guidance and direction through the writing process, especially if you are in a timed situation. Planning lets you see how your many developing ideas fit within a framework and clearly maps out the type of essay you are trying to write.

In this section, you'll learn planning strategies that will not only improve the effectiveness and quality of your writing, but will also help eliminate many of the frustrations writers face.

1 ▶ THINKING ABOUT AUDIENCE AND PURPOSE

LESSON SUMMARY

This lesson explains how knowing *why* and *for whom* you're writing helps improve its effectiveness.

There are few things in life students dread more than an essay assignment. But the essay prompt and the instructions to complete it are critical to your success: they are both the starting point for your ideas and your guide through the writing process. The more you've considered what is being asked of you, the clearer your task is—and the steps necessary to complete it. That first step is to understand *what* and *why* you are writing, and *for whom* you are being asked to write. Purpose and audience not only determine *how* you write; they shape your content.

For example, imagine you've just had this amazing experience: You were able to save someone's life by performing CPR. You want to share the experience with three people: your father, your best friend, and the admissions officer at your first-choice college. How will you describe what happened? Will that description be the same for each person? The likely answer is, probably not.

Although the subject remains a constant, each person is a different *audience*, requiring different word choices, levels of formality, and tone. Because you are sharing the experience with these three people for different reasons, the *purpose* of your description changes, too. You might tell your father to let him know that his advice about taking a CPR course was invaluable. To your friend, you might stress the emotions the experience evoked. In your college application essay, you place an emphasis on the experience's revelation of your competent and responsible nature.

Understanding Your Audience

The essay assignments found on college applications, AP exams, the SAT, and the ACT are designed to elicit essays that fulfill a specific need or purpose. In order to fulfill the assignment, you must understand exactly what the assignment is asking you to do. This may sound simple, but consider that many essay assignments aren't obvious. What does it mean, for example, to discuss an experience? How are you supposed to *analyze* an issue?

Breaking Down the Assignment

To understand an assignment, you first need to understand the following:

- What you need to respond to (the topic)
- How you are to respond to it

In some cases, there may be more than one topic and more than one way to respond. First, underline the words that *describe* the topic—look for keywords and phrases from your current course of study, or for repeated nouns and terms. Next, circle all of the verbs that tell you how to address the topic—e.g., *analyze, describe, discuss, explain, evaluate, identify, illustrate,* and *argue.*

For example, here is a writing assignment from an AP Biology exam:

Describe the chemical nature of genes. Discuss the replicative process of DNA in eukaryotic organisms. Be sure to include the various types of gene mutations that can occur during replication.

By breaking down the assignment, you can identify three subjects, each with its own direction word. The subjects are underlined and the direction words are circled:

(Describe) the chemical nature of genes. (Discuss) the replicative process of DNA in eukaryotic organisms. Be sure to (include) the various types of gene mutations that can occur during replication.

To help make the assignment even more manageable, break down the two parts (topic and direction words) into a simple chart:

Subject	Directions
1. The chemical nature of genes	describe
2. The replicative process of DNA in eukaryotic organisms	discuss
3. The various types of gene mutations that can occur during replication	include

To completely fulfill the assignment, you must cover all three of these subjects in the manner in which the assignment dictates.

Understanding Direction Words

You've broken down the assignment and isolated the direction words. But what do those direction words really mean? In the following table, you'll find the most common essay direction words and their explanations.

TERM	MEANING
Analyze	Divide the issue into its main parts and discuss each part. Consider how the parts interact and how they work together to form the whole.
Argue	Express your opinion about the subject, and support it with evidence, examples, and details.
Assess	See *evaluate*.
Classify	Organize the subject into groups and explain why the groupings make sense.
Compare	Point out similarities.
Contrast	Point out differences.
Define	Give the meaning of the subject.
Describe	Show readers what the subject is like; give an account of the subject.
Discuss	Point out the main issues or characteristics of the subject and elaborate.
Evaluate	Make a judgment about the effectiveness and success of the subject. What is good and bad about it? Why? Describe your criteria for your judgment.
Explain	Make your position, issue, process, etc. clear by analyzing, defining, comparing, contrasting, or illustrating.
Identify	Name and describe.
Illustrate	Provide examples of the subject.
Indicate	Explain what you think the subject means and how you came to that interpretation.
Relate	Point out and discuss any connections.
Summarize	Describe the main ideas or points.

Here are a few examples:

Compare and contrast prohibition and the current anti-tobacco movement.

This assignment gives you two direction words: *compare* and *contrast*. Therefore, you should locate and discuss the similarities and differences between the two subjects (prohibition and the anti-tobacco movement).

Rousseau offers judgments about the relative goodness and badness of life as a savage and of life in society. Assess the validity of these judgments. What arguments does he provide to support them? Are they sound arguments?

The explicit direction word in this assignment is *assess*. The implied direction word for the first question, "What arguments does he provide to support them?" is *identify*. The implied direction word for the second question, "Are they sound arguments?" is *evaluate*. For this assignment, you are expected to:

1. Assess the validity and soundness of Rousseau's judgments
2. Identify the arguments he uses to support his judgments
3. Evaluate the strengths and/or weaknesses of his argument

Practice 1

Read the essay topic carefully. Use the subject and directions columns in the tables provided to break them down into parts. (Note: You may not need to fill each table.)

Describe the change in citizens' attitudes toward the federal government in the last decade. Explain what you believe to be the causes of this change. Finally, assess the impact of this attitude on the power of the government.

SUBJECT	DIRECTIONS

When the Assignment is a Question

In some assignments, you are given questions instead of direction words. Here's an example:

What were the issues, successes, and failures of the Civil Rights movement from the 1960s through the 1970s?

Notice that there are no direction words. For this type of essay prompt, you will need to determine the word(s) yourself. Reread the question, paying careful attention to each word. Notice it begins with *What were*. This is a good clue that you should *identify* the issues, successes, and failures.

Translating questions into directions can be tricky, but it's a critical step in understanding the prompt. You need to determine exactly how you're supposed to respond to the subject. The following chart lists common question words and corresponding direction words.

QUESTION WORDS	WHAT THEY USUALLY MEAN
What is/are . . .	define or identify
What caused . . .	identify or explain
How are/does . . .	explain or evaluate
How is X like . . .	compare
How is X different . . .	contrast
In what way . . .	illustrate
Do you agree?	argue
Why is/does . . .	explain
What do you think of X?	evaluate

Practice 2

Read the essay topic carefully. Use the subject and directions columns in the table provided to break the topic down into parts. (Note: You may not need to fill each table.)

In Alice Walker's novel The Color Purple, *does Celie have control over her destiny? Explain your answer.*

SUBJECT	DIRECTIONS

Knowing Your Purpose

Analyzing an assignment task helps to not only clarify the requirements, but also helps you define your own goal(s) for what you hope to convey in writing. To help you clarify your purpose, you can try completing a simple fill-in-the-blank:

My goal in this essay is to _____

_____

Try to find a verb or verbs that best describe what you want your essay to do; the "Understanding Direction Words" table on page 21 can help. Notice in the following example how the verb specifies purpose and subject matter:

My goal is to *prove* that Victor Frankenstein, rather than his creature, is the monster.

Think of a goal statement as a preliminary thesis: By indicating what you want to achieve and how you will go about doing so, you've articulated the main idea of your writing.

Practice 3

Review the instructions for an essay you have recently been assigned. How would you describe your purpose? Write a goal statement that expresses what purpose your essay will attempt to achieve and how.

_____

_____

Understanding Your Audience

At the beginning of the lesson, you were asked to consider how to communicate the experience of using CPR to save a life to three very different people—your father, your best friend, and an admissions officer. Now imagine that you've been asked to write about your experience for the local hospital newsletter. You expect your audience to be adults, so you'll need to plan and draft your article in anticipation of that audience.

What are the likely characteristics, needs, and wants of the audience reading the hospital newsletter? Fill out the audience analysis chart below.

Audience Analysis: Hospital Newsletter	
Characteristics of Audience	Needs or Wants of Audience

When you submit it, you find that the hospital plans to use your article in a supplement for elementary school students. Can they print it as written? Perhaps not if they want their readers to understand what you've written. You'll likely need to plan and draft your article to meet the needs of your young audience.

What are the likely characteristics and needs or wants of the audience reading the elementary school supplement to the hospital newsletter? Fill out the audience analysis chart below.

Audience Analysis: Elementary School Student Supplement to Hospital Newsletter	
Characteristics of Audience	Needs or Wants of Audience

Knowing Your Audience

As the previous exercise illustrates, a writer cannot begin to achieve his or her purpose for writing until it is clear who the reader is and what his or her needs are. *Who* will read your essay, and *why* are they reading it? *What* do they know about your subject?

Here are some general guidelines:

WHO THEY ARE	WHAT THEY'RE LOOKING FOR
Admission officer	an engaging essay that reveals your personality, goals, and values; evidence that you can organize your thoughts and communicate effectively
SAT and ACT scorers	a polished rough draft that responds to the topic, develops a point of view, and supports that point of view with examples and evidence
AP exam evaluators	a clear and cohesive essay that demonstrates mastery of the subject matter
High school teachers	a combination of the following: mastery of the material (do you understand the book, concept, issue?); a clear and original thesis; mastery of standard written English

Although they differ in many ways, these audiences share the same purpose for reading: to *evaluate*. Your writing is being used to assess your competency—your ability to demonstrate an understanding of coursework, your readiness for college-level work, etc. Given this purpose, what are they looking for when evaluating your writing? Think about it for a minute. This last question is especially important when writing an essay; you need to know the expectations in order to fulfill them.

What does your English teacher consider an A essay? How does a college admissions officer judge an essay? For the SAT and ACT, what are the differences between an essay that gets a 6, and one that gets a 2? Understanding your role as a writer and the role of the reader helps determine the style, tone, and format of your essay.

In this case, consider the essay evaluator: he or she likely knows a great deal about your subject, is looking for a fully developed and well-reasoned argument, and expects that the directions of the assignment and of formal writing in general are to be followed throughout the response. No text messaging language here; you'll need lots of clear, detailed, and specific evidence.

Consider what must be done to achieve the essay purpose and reach the intended audience—that is, what it will take to get an A, a 6, or accepted by a college—and use it to create the framework or map to guide your planning and drafting. In many cases, your reader has provided a guide that states his or her expectations—a scoring guide or rubric. In the case of college application essays, The College Board (the publishers of the SAT and AP exams) publishes sample essays at www.collegeboard.com/student/apply/essay-skills/. Review their rubrics carefully. With a clear purpose and an understanding of what is expected of you, you can know where you need to be!

Practice 4

Think about a class you are currently taking, one in which writing is an important part of the coursework. What are the essential characteristics of grade-A essay work in this class? What must you do in your writing to fulfill the expectations of the teacher? Write down your thoughts on the following lines.

_____

_____

_____

_____

_____

In Short

Effective writing begins with a clear understanding of purpose and audience. Break down the writing assignment so you can clearly grasp your evaluator's expectations. As always, know your audience: *who* will read your essay? Consider your relationship to your readers, and be sure to carefully consider your purpose.

Skill Building Practice

Review sample ACT student essays at actstudent.org/writing/sample/index.html, and SAT essays at sat.collegeboard.com/scores/sat-essay-scoring-guide, focusing on those that scored 6. What makes these exemplary essays? What will you need to work on in order to meet these expectations?

2 ▶ WHAT TO WRITE ABOUT

LESSON SUMMARY

This lesson explains how to narrow your topic so that it is sufficiently focused. You'll also learn how to develop a tentative thesis for your essay.

You've established your purpose, identified your audience, and identified what's expected of you. It's time to take the next step. Regardless of whether you can choose what to write about, or are just given a specific question to address, every writer starts out with big—and often broad—ideas.

A junior is assigned a research essay on a topic of his choosing; he may want to write on topics like social networking, capital punishment, genetic engineering—interesting, sure, but likely too sizable for the task. An ACT test taker is prompted to take a side on a specific education-related issue, but has not taken a stand on the topic before: she has some basic ideas, but lacks reasons and specific evidence to formulate a complete position. Writers need to funnel their topics before generating ideas and starting to draft their essays, in order to narrow their focus and create a clear vision. Funneling leads to a very helpful outcome—an initial thesis.

Finding a Focus

Essay assignments often ask you to write about a very broad subject area. For example, your topic might be to write about the Cold War or about a novel you read in class. Even if the assignment is more specific or directed, chances are you still have some degree of choice—what position to take, what ideas to focus on over others, what evidence to use, and so on.

These choices enable your voice and unique ideas to be articulated, and focus is required if your essay is to be successful.

A research report on genetic engineering, for instance, will need a specific issue or idea within that broad topic—how genetic engineering may be used to find cures for diseases, create super crops, or plan a family with designer children—if it is to be adequately covered within the confines of the essay. If you try to cover too much, you'll have to briefly mention many subtopics, without delving into the core of your topic.

Suppose you were composing a response to the following essay assignment:

Assignment: Write a statement for your generation.

Start by identifying the general topic for your response.
- Broad topic: My generation
  - That's a broad topic: a generation has many defining traits, not to mention millions of members. You'll have to ask yourself, "well, what about my generation?" Start by identifying one key aspect of this topic that interests you.
- Narrowed topic: My generation's beliefs
  - This at least helps you clarify that you'll be writing about values and not, say, shoes. Still, your generation has a lot of beliefs. What issue or topic will you focus on?
- Further narrowed topic: My generation's beliefs about work
  - Better, but which beliefs about work are you particularly interested? When you think about what could be written about (the kinds of jobs available, working from home vs. working in an office, etc.), you realize that the subtopics are still big enough to be essays on their own. Let's try to pinpoint a specific belief.
- Sufficiently narrowed topic: My generation's beliefs about the balance between work and play
  - Here's a specific belief with plenty to examine, yet focused enough to explore sufficiently in a short paper. Good topic!

Notice how several stages of refining take place in order to drill down to an appropriate topic statement.

Practice 1

Using the following assignment, funnel your topic so that it is sufficiently focused.

Assignment:	Write a research essay that takes and supports a stand on an important issue currently impacting American society.
Broad topic:	
Narrowed topic:	
Further narrowed topic:	
Sufficiently narrowed topic:	

Turning Your Topic into a Question

In the previous example, the essay topic was narrowed down to *my generation's beliefs about the balance between work and play*. To come up with a thesis, you can restate that topic in the form of a question: What are my generation's beliefs about the balance between work and play? The answer to that question might be, *My generation believes that life should be made up of equal parts of work and play*.

Here are two more examples of the evolution of a tentative thesis from an assignment, a focused topic, and a question.

Assignment:	Describe how you think the federal income tax system should be reformed and why.
Broad topic:	Reforming the federal tax system
Narrowed topic:	Problems with the federal tax system
Further narrowed topic:	Inequalities in the federal tax system
Sufficiently narrowed topic:	How to eliminate inequalities in the federal tax system
Topic turned into a question:	How can we eliminate inequalities in the federal tax system?
Tentative thesis:	Instituting a flat tax will eliminate inequalities.

Assignment:	Write an essay that explores one of the many issues raised in *Frankenstein*.
Broad topic:	An issue in Frankenstein
Narrowed topic:	Responsibility
Sufficiently narrowed topic:	Responsibility of the creator to his creation
Topic turned into a question:	What is the responsibility of the creator to his creation?
Tentative thesis:	If the creation is a living being, then the creator is responsible for nurturing and educating his "child."

Practice 2

For the following assignment, identify a broad topic, narrow it, and turn it into a question and tentative thesis.

Assignment:	Identify a factor that you believe figures strongly in a child's personality development. Explain how that factor may influence the child.
Broad topic:	
Narrowed topic:	
Further narrowed topic:	
Sufficiently narrowed topic:	
Topic turned into a question:	
Tentative thesis:	

Practice 3

Use the table below to select and narrow a topic for an upcoming essay assignment or timed writing essay practice.

Assignment:	
Broad topic:	
Narrowed topic:	
Further narrowed topic:	
Sufficiently narrowed topic:	
Topic turned into a question:	
Tentative thesis:	

In Short

To write an effective essay, your topic must be sufficiently focused so that the amount of material you cover can be adequately explored within the confines of an essay. Funnel your topic until you can turn it into a specific question. The answer to this question should serve as your tentative thesis—the main idea that you will address and develop in your essay.

Skill Building Practice

Choose topics and develop tentative thesis statements for any of the sample assignments featured in the Introduction or Chapter 1.

3 ▶ BRAINSTORMING TECHNIQUES: LOOPING AND FORCED CHOICE/TWO— COLUMN NOTES

LESSON SUMMARY

Even the most experienced writers sometimes have trouble coming up with ideas. This lesson teaches you two important techniques for generating ideas.

How seriously should you take brainstorming? For many writers, taking the time to generate and articulate ideas before organizing and drafting a response seems wasteful and irrelevant; after all, if they already know what they think, why write it down twice?

Unfortunately for those writers, the lack of quality time spent honing a thought becomes all too evident in their essay, and leads to an overly simplistic thesis, a lack of specific evidence or details, and a higher risk of language errors that make understanding the writer's ideas more difficult.

The bottom line—brainstorming is important. The key is to utilize a brainstorming strategy that you feel will help you generate better ideas. The next few lessons present four focused strategies to help you develop and clarify your thoughts—use the one that works best for you!

Looping

Looping is a kind of structured writing that both encourages free-form writing on a topic and prompts the writer to focus on the value and potential of emerging ideas. The writer starts by taking time to write continuously on an established writing topic, usually 5 to 10 minutes. At the completion of this period, the writer takes one to two minutes to review her efforts, and selects a key sentence or phrase she generated to explore further. This becomes the start of a new, shorter round of free writing (three to five minutes). The process can continue until the basic essay components (thesis, support, et al.) emerge.

Example

A student receives the following essay assignment:

Assignment: *Adrienne Rich wrote: "Lying is done with words and also with silence." Do you agree? Use your personal experience and/or your observations to support your answer.*

Here is the result of a short freewriting session:

Do I agree? I think so. Is it a lie if you don't say something when you know something? Not technically, but it has the same effect, doesn't it? I remember when I saw Jay with someone else but I didn't tell Karen. She never came out and asked me if Jay was cheating on her, but I knew. But that's not really a lie is it, so what do you call it? But there are more important cases where not telling the truth can be deadly. Like if you know someone is planning to commit a crime, and you don't tell anyone. Didn't someone go to jail for not telling the police she knew about the Oklahoma City bombing before it happened? But that's not a lie, it's just not telling, so not telling is not the same as lying. But it can have equally terrible consequences. I guess the point is that you know a truth but you don't reveal it. So they're not the same but they do the same thing. People can get hurt. Unless you believe what you don't know won't hurt you. But that probably falls into the same category as a white lie. It's the other lies and other silences that are the problem.

During her free writing session, this student started to develop a position and came up with a couple of good examples. Her definition and classification of lies gives her a foundation to build her position, and a good place for idea generation: she has circled the last sentence because she has identified but not yet fully explained why other lies are the problem.

Practice 1

Using a separate sheet of paper or your computer, spend five minutes free writing on the following essay assignment. Remember, there is no wrong answer for this exercise; just be sure to address the topic provided. Keep working, don't stop, and don't edit or judge.

Assignment: *In his essay, "Urban Strategy," William Rhoden describes a time that he put himself at risk to do what he thought was right. Describe a time when you, like Rhoden, put yourself at risk (physically, socially, emotionally, and/or academically) to do what you thought was right. Was it worth the risk? Why or why not?*

Once the time is up, review your work and select a sentence or phrase on which to write further. Spend an additional five minutes free writing again, and continue the process until you feel as though you've developed a solid foundation.

Although the looping process is more ideally suited for essay assignments for which you're given several days or weeks to complete, shortened two to three minute bursts of looping can be very effective on writing exams, even those as short as the ACT.

Forced Choice and Two-Column Notes

Students typically brainstorm by creating a list of ideas and short phrases they associate with a topic. Usually, this list (particularly on ACT and SAT essays) merely identifies the two or three topics the student will address in his/her body paragraphs. Not very useful. A simple two-step process can help—it will narrow your focus and help you begin to organize and expand the ideas most suited for your essay.

Start as you would any ordinary brainstorm. Take two to three minutes to list all of the ideas you can think of on your topic. When time is up, review the list and conduct a *forced choice*—select and highlight the three or four most significant ideas on your list as the key ideas you are likely to explore in your essay.

Next, make a two-column chart, with *key ideas* in the left column and *support* in the right. Place your key ideas in the rows of the left column. For support, brainstorm and list possible reasons, details, and/or evidence that help support your ideas.

In the following example, a student first conducts a forced choice to generate ideas for his college application essay.

Assignment: **In your opinion, what is the greatest challenge your generation will face? What ideas do you have for dealing with this issue?**

- Being overwhelmed by technology
- How will we know what's real?
- Find better ways to take care of parents and grandparents
- Being overwhelmed by information
- What about the people who don't have access to technology—social inequality
- The environment
- Come up with alternative fuel sources
- Disease—new viruses—bird flu?
- What about our new power for destruction, biowarfare?

As you can see, the student has a lot of potential directions, some quite similar and others rather disparate. Upon reviewing his findings, he sees that the negative effects of technology seem to be an emerging concern in several of his ideas and selects three challenges that express this concern. Next, he uses two-column notes to address the two parts of the assignment—explaining why the idea is a challenge to the world, and offering a potential solution to the problem.

KEY IDEAS	SUPPORT
Being overwhelmed by technology	Young people today lack key social experiences, suffering greater stress and emotional upheaval **Solution:** more technology in classroom; more promotion of non-tech leisure activities
Being overwhelmed by information	People are more susceptible to and accepting of erroneous or misleading information; no longer critical consumers of information
Inequitable access to technology	Those with less access to technology also have less access to good jobs, good schools Free wi-fi in impoverished areas; more job training in technology careers for urban students

In addition to developing a number of supporting details, notice how this process also helps solidify the thesis or main idea of the essay—that the overabundance of technology will have a negative effect on social interaction and quality of life.

Practice 2

Take three to five minutes to brainstorm a list of ideas for the following assignment:

Assignment: *Many forces contribute to our sense of self. What are strong determining factors for your sense of identity?*

- When you are finished, select three or four key ideas.
- Complete the two-column notes for these ideas in the following table.
- Review your notes and develop a preliminary thesis based on your ideas.

Key Ideas	Support

Summary

Two effective ways to generate ideas and clarify your thinking, beyond what you already know, are structured free writing (looping) and listing (forced choice/two-column notes) techniques.

- By emphasizing and refocusing ideas from your free writing, looping helps writers ask, "What does this mean?"
- By emphasizing the listing and organizing of main ideas and supporting details, using forced choice and two-column notes helps writers identify what they can write about, as well as what is important to their responses.

Skill Building Practice

Use the looping and forced choice/two-column notes techniques to help define your perspective on a current event or national issue of recent prominence. Use looping to free write about the pros and cons. Use forced choice/two-column notes to identify and support your position.

4 ▶ BRAINSTORMING TECHNIQUES: CUBING

LESSON SUMMARY

This lesson describes a technique for generating ideas for your essays: cubing.

People learn and process information in many different ways. Some of us learn best by seeing, others by hearing, and still others by doing. Some of us prefer a defined structure or framework, while others think best when there are no constraints. For those who like structure, cubing offers an easy framework for generating ideas. For visual learners and thinkers, graphic organization tools like cubing work best.

Cubing

The beauty of cubing is the depth of questioning it asks the writer to undertake in order to fully grasp the essay topic. To complete a "cube" of an assignment is to think critically, consider multiple perspectives, solve problems, and take a stand—all in ten minutes!

How does it work? Think of each side of a cube as a question: six questions, six different sides to a topic. A writer would consider everything she knows and/or believes about a topic in response to the following series of questions:

CUBING DIRECTIONS
Describe: What do you know about the topic?
Compare: How is your topic related to other school or societal issues? How does it differ?
Associate: What does the topic make you think of? Perhaps people? Places? Things? Feelings?
Analyze: What are the topic's traits and attributes? What causes it? What effect(s) does it have?
Apply: What would happen if the task topic occurred (or did not occur)? What would happen if the topic was changed in some way?
Argue: Where do you stand on the topic? Why?

Here's how cubing might look on a typical ACT writing assignment:

Assignment: *Should high schools offer money or rewards as an incentive to increase student academic performance? Defend your position.*

CUBING EXAMPLE	
Cubing Steps	**Responses**
Describe:	I know they've tried this in cities and in schools that are having problems; I think the cash amounts they give out are pretty low—$100 or so.
Compare:	This reminds me of awards ceremonies, but will cash or prizes help less motivated students the way awards might motivate more eager students? Those students are in it for more than a gala dinner, though, so I wonder if $100 will be enough.
Associate:	I hear a lot about test scores these days, and in the past I've spent weeks in the spring taking tests we were told were important; I saw a lot of my peers not try hard or not finish because it didn't matter to them. Maybe an iPod or cash would have helped.
Analyze:	I'm thinking the interest in rewards came about as an attempt to improve test scores at lower-performing schools. I bet there was a lot of early buzz, but staying focused on school is tough; I wonder if they had to offer extra incentives as the school year progressed.
Apply:	If incentives were to be offered at my school for better grades or test scores, I could see a number of my classmates looking into it; it would take a much bigger payout, however, to get more students interested. I'd say $1,000 would be the magic number.
Argue:	Even if only a few people do better in a school because of a reward, it would still be worth it. Still, I think you can't offer a prize without also offering extra help—tutoring, for instance.

Notice how the number of steps not only enabled the student to generate a significant amount of possible essay material, but also allowed her to draw connections to both the real world and her own world, connections she used to formulate what should be a nuanced thesis. In the next lesson, you'll learn how to use a brainstorming session like this to develop a thesis and organize your essay ideas.

Practice 1

Use the cubing technique to generate ideas for the following assignment.

Assignment: School uniforms for public school students is among the most controversial proposals for education reform in America. Where do you stand on this issue? Defend your position.

CUBING DIRECTIONS

Describe:

Compare:

Associate:

Analyze:

Apply:

Argue:

Skill Building Practice

Review a sample ACT or SAT writing assignment and brainstorm a response by using the cubing technique to generate ideas in response; give yourself no more than seven minutes to complete the task. Afterward, reflect on how effective your brainstorming with cubing was. Is cubing an appropriate brainstorming technique on shorter writing examinations such as these? What method is the best fit for you? Why?

5 ▶ DEVELOPING A THESIS

LESSON SUMMARY

This lesson explains how to develop a strong thesis for your essay.

As with the other pre-drafting lessons in this guide, crafting an effective thesis statement provides and ensures focus. It not only articulates your main idea but also serves as a constant reminder of the goal and purpose of your essay. With an effective thesis statement, every decision you make while drafting can be determined by the answer to a simple question: *Does it support my thesis?* Think of it as your goal, your reminder of what it will take to turn a thesis into an effective essay. But how do you write one? This is the focus of this lesson.

The Role of the Thesis Statement

Suppose you were asked to write an essay in which you argued whether or not the United States was losing its superpower status. Setting aside your personal beliefs on the question, which of these examples best reflects what you believe a strong thesis is?

- **Example #1:** I do not agree that America is in decline.
- **Example #2:** The fact that America represents 25% of the world's entire economy yet only has 5% of its population is proof that it is hardly in decline.
- **Example #3:** If America is in decline, it is not because of a loss of economic or military power, but because our nation no longer represents and reflects the values that the world's people once believed we championed.
- **Example #4:** On one hand, some writers believe that America still commands the world's attention and respect; other writers argue that the country is facing a political and moral decline.

The best choice is Example #3. It is argumentative, focused, and detailed. Let's consider why these traits are critical to a strong thesis.

An Argumentative Thesis

Your **thesis** is the main idea of your essay—and your main idea is the primary point you are trying to convince others of. Think of your thesis in terms of persuasion—a good thesis makes a strong, clear statement about your beliefs and attitude about the essay subject. Consider these examples:

No argument:	*The School of Rock* is about a substitute teacher.
Mild argument:	*The School of Rock* is an entertaining film about an influential substitute teacher.
Strong argument:	*The School of Rock* derives much of its charm from the way it both parodies and reveres rock musicians.

Let's suppose this is a movie review. Given the purpose of such a piece of writing (to evaluate), the first statement is merely a fact from the movie; it's hardly a main idea, and hardly a full essay on the film. The second does state an opinion (*entertaining*) but gives us little else—the writer is entitled to his/her enjoyment, but what is there to discuss? What about the third statement? A reader could question it, believing the characterization of the schoolchildren or Jack Black's unbridled performance to be the driving force of the movie. It is the strongest argument because it takes a firm position regarding an idea that can hold multiple points of view.

A Focused Thesis

The previous example illustrates the need for a good thesis statement to strike the right balance between too broad and too narrow. When a thesis statement is too broad, it often fails to capture the actual focus in the body paragraphs, or it isn't an argument at all. If it is too narrow, the writer might not be able to fully address the assignment.

Consider the following examples:

Too broad:	**Animals have developed many strategies for survival.**
Some focus:	**Animals have developed many strategies to protect themselves.**
Focused:	**Animals with well-developed physical properties are most protected from predators.**
Too narrow:	**In "The Open Boat," the repetition of "If I am going to be drowned" conveys Crane's theme of the indifference of nature.**
Balanced:	**In "The Open Boat," Crane uses repetition and figurative language to convey his theme of the indifference of nature.**

In the first examples, the term *many strategies* is so vague as to make the statement incontestable; the too narrow version using "The Open Boat" is merely a specific example of the author's use of language, and would be difficult to discuss extensively.

A Detailed Thesis

No discussion of thesis statements is complete without the following mantra: *show, don't tell*. Earlier, we said that the thesis statement is your guide to your paper; it is not, however, simply an announcement of the subject matter. Consider this example:

This paper will discuss some of the erroneous theories about the causes of the Great Depression.

What's wrong with this picture? It's a table of contents, really, not an indication of what matters. The only thing that could be proved is whether or not the writer did discuss the theories—but we know that's not what she meant. A better thesis would surely show the fundamental idea behind the writer's thinking:

The Great Depression was caused neither by the stock market crash of 1929 nor the Smoot Hawley Tariff Act.

An effective thesis statement also cannot be a question. Remember, you are taking a position on the essay topic, not deflecting that decision to the reader. Devising the question your essay will answer is a helpful early step, but it is your answer to that question, not the question itself, that is your thesis. Consider the following example:

Question: Why did Kafka choose to turn Gregor into a giant beetle?

Thesis statement: Gregor's transformation into a giant beetle is a powerful symbol, representing his industrious nature and his role in his family, both before and after his transformation.

Practice 1

Revise and improve the following weak thesis statements.

1. The death penalty is a controversial issue.

_____

2. What would the consequences of censorship on the Internet be?

_____

Drafting a Thesis Statement

There's no single magic formula for creating a thesis; a thesis arises from the purpose, audience, and topic of your essay, and that always changes. However, you know what a good thesis statement is, and this section will work with you to articulate it just right.

Try gathering the essentials of what you know, and form a one-paragraph mini-essay regarding where you currently stand. The following template can help:

My goal with this essay is to _____. My own view is that _____ because _____. Though I concede that _____, I still maintain that _____. For example, _____. Although some might object that_____, I reply that _____. The issue is important because _____.

Using this template will help you generate a main idea, some reasons in support or concession of your position, and an understanding of what's at stake. The next step is to extract from this articulation the principal idea and rationale that is likely to guide your writing. For example, suppose the essay topic was on whether his/her school should require students to wear uniforms

My goal with this essay is to _convince the school board that a uniform code won't solve our school's problems._ My own view is that _school dress codes should not be a priority to change because clothing does not impact our ability to learn._ Though I concede that _certain clothing items can be inappropriate, distracting, and controversial,_ I still maintain that _the number of instances where clothes caused serious problems at our school is minimal._ For example, _the principal is very quick to catch students who dress inappropriately; he makes them change clothes immediately, and very few students are exposed to the problem._ Although some might object that _I am too easily excusing the behaviors of young people,_ I reply that _the school administrators are focusing on an issue that won't improve the school academically._ The issue is important because _it defines whether our school prioritizes learning and growth or whether it is merely interested in discipline._

A quick review of the writing reveals an emerging main idea: requiring students to wear uniforms wouldn't improve the school's ability to help its students learn; therefore, it is a proposal that should not be enacted. The writer will want to articulate that statement more formally, so let's look at a template that can help us compose a formal thesis statement:

Position Thesis

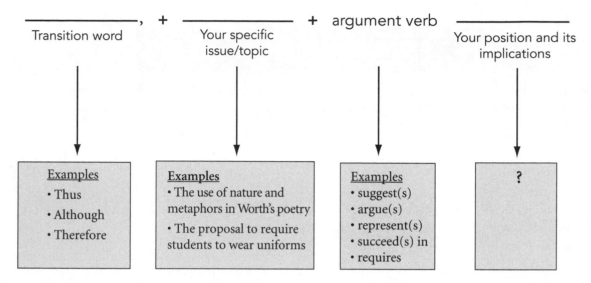

This template is structured to ensure that the key components of an effective thesis—a focused description of your topic and a clear position—are present, but it doesn't have to be followed exactly. Try playing around with the format to see if you can generate two possible thesis statements for the writer's ideas.

Possible Thesis #1: _____

Possible Thesis #2: _____

Of course, your thesis may change depending on the development of your essay. Regardless, it puts you in the position to begin outlining the structure of your essay and determining how you will support the stated position.

Practice 2

Earlier, you were presented with example thesis statements on *The School of Rock*, a comedy film. Suppose you were asked to evaluate a recent film you watched for its thematic and/or aesthetic value. Complete the following practice assignment:

1. Describe the purpose of a film review and the characteristics/needs of the audience (e.g., a teacher or evaluator of writing) when reading a film review.
2. Identify your topic, including both the film and what particular aspects of it you will discuss. Compose a goal statement.
3. Use cubing or mapping to develop ideas on what your review will discuss.
4. Use templates to compose an initial thesis for the response.

Summary

As the frame or guide for your writing, a thesis statement must be argumentative, focused, and detailed to be effective. Experiment with the ideas and structure of your thesis by using templates to help shape your ideas.

Skill Building Practice

Read a couple of essays and look for their thesis statements. How do the authors convey their main ideas? Where are the thesis statements located?

6 ▶ OUTLINING AND ORGANIZATIONAL STRATEGIES

LESSON SUMMARY

In this lesson, you'll learn about the underlying structure of an essay and how to create an outline. We'll also examine some of the common organizational strategies used by essay writers.

The Assertion → Support Structure

Before discussing common organizational strategies, it's important to consider the underlying structure of essays. Whether an essay is organized by chronology, comparison and contrast, cause and effect, or some other strategy, every essay has the same underlying structure:

$$assertion \rightarrow support$$

An essay **asserts** an idea (its thesis) and then **supports** the thesis with specific examples, evidence, and details. These supports form the body paragraphs of your essay, and the general structure looks the same nearly every time:

- **Topic sentence** that states the main idea of the paragraph
- **Evidence** that supports main idea
- **Explanation** of how evidence supports the topic sentence
- **Concluding statement** that articulates how the provided support proves the thesis

The exact underlying structure will vary, depending upon the number and type of supporting ideas, but this is the structural foundation for most high school essays.

The Benefits of an Outline

When done effectively, an outline bridges the gap between your ideas and an initial essay draft. Generating an outline not only gives structure to your ideas, but also allows you to structure these ideas in a way that reflects your expectations for writing, including content and organization. Because effective outlines require specific, supporting details and several levels of support, you'll know instantly if there are any gaps in the thesis or ideas of your work.

Here's an example of a detailed outline:

Assignment: *Evaluate the proposal to replace the current graded income tax system with a flat tax. Should we institute a flat tax system? Why or why not?*

I. Problems with the current system
   A. complex
      1. tax rates vary greatly
      2. too many intricate details
   B. unfair
      1. deductions, loopholes, special interests
      2. people with same income can pay different amount of taxes
   C. wasteful
      1. different forms for different people
      2. huge administrative costs
      3. huge compliance costs
      4. advising costs
II. How flat tax works
   A. all citizens pay same rate—17%—for income over a set minimum
   B. all citizens get same personal exemption
   C. no breaks for special interests
   D. no loopholes
III. Benefits
   A. citizens
      1. sense of fairness—all treated equally
      2. poorest pay no taxes
      3. simple to calculate and file
      4. families save more
      5. more faith in government
      6. people will save and invest more

B. government
  1. streamline IRS
    a. reduce cost
      i. fewer employees
      ii. less paper, printing, etc.
      iii. less auditing costs
  2. healthier economy

Common Organizational Strategies

Essay organization doesn't stop with the underlying **assertion → support** structure and an outline. A number of effective strategies can be used to organize your information and ideas, and bring a logical, easy-to-understand flow to your essay.

Chronological/Sequential

One way to organize your material is by **chronology**, or **time sequence**. Put ideas in the order in which they happened, should happen, or will happen. This method works best when you are narrating or describing an experience, procedure, or process. Imagine writing about the way a bill is passed in Congress, but the steps needed to complete the process are out of chronological or sequential order. The point or points you are trying to make about that process will get lost in the confusion.

Here is a sample rough outline using chronology as its organizing principle:

Assignment: *Describe a time when you and a family member experienced a deep sense of conflict or when you sharply disagreed about an important issue. What caused the conflict? What was the outcome? Have your feelings about the matter changed or remained the same? Explain.*

Tentative thesis: *When I decided to become a vegetarian, my parents refused to support me. It was very difficult to stick to my decision—but I'm glad I did.*

Outline:
  1. telling my family
  2. their reactions
  3. trying to explain my reasons
  4. flashback: taking the "virtual tour" of the slaughterhouse on the Web
  5. offering to take my family on the tour, but only Wei watching it with me
  6. Mom and Dad refusing to cook special meals for me
  7. learning to cook for myself
  8. Wei accepting my decision and trying some vegetarian meals with me
  9. Wei giving up meat too
  10. Mom and Dad accepting our decision and supporting us

Practice 1

On a separate sheet of paper or your computer, create an essay outline using chronology as your organizational principle. Use one of your brainstorms from Lesson 3 or 4, or one of the brainstorms provided to create your outline.

Order of Importance

One of the most frequently used organizational strategies, **order of importance** is often the main organizing principle of an essay. Even when it's not, it's often used in individual sections and paragraphs. You can begin with the most important idea, and work towards the least, or begin with the least important, and finish with the most. *Most important* generally means *most supportive*, *most convincing*, or *most striking*.

Suppose you were asked to describe the various strategies that organisms have developed for protection, with one of your major ideas being that some animals use their physical appearance to avoid threats. Consider how the writer would develop this concept in an outline:

I. Appearance
   A. camouflage
      1. moths
      2. flounder
      3. walking stick
   B. warning colors
      1. monarch butterfly
      2. coral snake
      3. South American poisonous frog
   C. mimicry
      1. king snake resembling coral snake
      2. swallowtail butterfly larva resembling snake
      3. snowberry fly resembling jumping spider

The three minor supporting ideas—camouflage, warning colors, and mimicry—are listed in order of importance. *Camouflage* is the most common and least sophisticated of the three, whereas *mimicry* is the most unique and most compelling way that animals use appearance for protection. For each of these three supporting ideas, three specific examples are provided. Again, they are listed in order of importance, from the least striking example to the most compelling.

Spatial

Ideas can also be organized according to **spatial** principles—from top to bottom, side to side, or inside to outside, for example. This organizational method is particularly useful when you are describing an item or place. You'd use this strategy to describe the structure of an animal or plant, the room where an important event took place, or a place that is important to you.

The key to using spatial organization effectively is to move around the space or object logically. Remember, you are using words to relate something that exists physically or visually and must help your reader understand your ideas.

What follows is a rough outline for an essay using the spatial organizing principle. The student works from the outside of a cell to the inside as she describes its structure:

I. Structure of an animal cell
  A. plasma membrane
    1. isolates cytoplasm
    2. regulates flow of materials between cytoplasm and environment
    3. allows interaction with other cells
  B. cytoplasm
    1. contains water, salt, enzymes, proteins
    2. also contains organelles like mitochondria
  C. nuclear envelope
    1. protects nucleus
    2. regulates flow of materials between nucleus and cystoplasm
  D. nucleus
    1. contains cell's DNA
    2. regulates gene expression

Practice 2

On a separate sheet of paper or on your computer, create an outline using either the order of importance or spatial organizing principle. Use one of your brainstorms from Lesson 5, or one of the brainstorms provided, to create your outline.

Summary

Organizing your ideas to create an effective essay can be done on a number of different levels. Underlying all essays is the **assertion → support** structure. For every idea or assertion you make, you need to provide examples, evidence, and details as support.

An outline provides a roadmap that not only helps you in the drafting process, but also lets you see where your ideas may need more development or support. Within an outline, ideas can be arranged using a number of strategies. Chronology or time sequence, order of importance, and spatial arrangements can be used, based on the type of information you are writing about and the purpose of your writing.

Skill Building Practice

In a well-organized essay, a writer's organizing principle should be very clear. Find an essay from your schoolwork that incorporates chronological, order of importance, or spatial principles. Develop an outline from the text so you can see the organizational structure clearly.

7 ▶ MORE ORGANIZATIONAL STRATEGIES

LESSON SUMMARY

This lesson describes four more organizational strategies for essays: **classification**, **comparison and contrast**, **cause and effect**, and **problem → solution**.

In the previous lesson, you learned ways to organize ideas according to time and space. Now, you'll examine four additional principles of organization:

1. classification
2. comparison and contrast
3. cause and effect
4. problem → solution

Classification

Some essays are best organized by arranging ideas, items, or events by their characteristics or functions. The following assignment is broad enough to describe many different strategies.

Assignment: *Plants and animals protect themselves in many different ways. Describe the various strategies organisms have developed for protection.*

It makes sense to group similar strategies together and organize your essay by type (classification). A formal outline to address the assignment might look like this:

I. Appearance
  A. camouflage
    1. moths
    2. flounder
    3. walking stick
  B. warning colors
    1. monarch butterfly
    2. coral snake
    3. South American poisonous frog
  C. mimicry
    1. king snake resembling coral snake
    2. swallowtail butterfly larva resembling snake
    3. snowberry fly resembling jumping spider

II. Chemicals
  A. smoke
    1. squid
    2. octopus
  B. smells
    1. skunks
    2. others?
  C. poisons
    1. spiders
    2. snakes
    3. bombardier beetles

III. Armor
  A. spikes, thorns
    1. roses and thistles
    2. sea urchins
    3. porcupines
  B. shells, hard coverings
    1. nuts
    2. beetles
    3. turtles

Notice how the protective strategies are first classified into three categories: appearance, chemicals, and armor. Each of these categories is then further classified for analysis. Appearance, for example, is broken down into three types of protection strategies: camouflage, warning colors, and mimicry.

Comparison and Contrast

Essays that show the similarities and differences between two or more ideas typically use the comparison and contrast organizational strategy. This strategy depends upon first having comparable ideas or items.

For example, you'd have difficulty writing a successful essay if you wanted to compare Frankenstein's creature with Cinderella. Frankenstein's creature and Pinocchio, on the other hand, are comparable items—they're both beings that someone else brought to life. Often, comparable items have a number of aspects that may be compared and contrasted. You might compare and contrast the creation of the figures, their creators' reactions after they come to life, and/or their relationships with their creators.

In grade school, you were likely asked to make simple comparisons of known ideas—one paragraph for cats, another for dogs, for example. However, in high school and college writing it is not enough to simply list the traits of the things being compared. The purpose of advanced comparison and contrast writing is to uncover what meaning and relevance arises from setting two or more things against one another. Therefore, when an essay assignment prompts you to compare or contrast, you should ask yourself: *What is the key idea that connects the two or more things to be compared?*

For our Pinocchio/Frankenstein example, the comparisons could yield some interesting conclusions about the ethics of scientific creation. These can only emerge if your writing is organized by the aspect or concept that links the compared phenomena, rather than separating and resulting in a direct comparison and contrast (known as the point-by-point technique). Because you put each aspect side by side, readers get to see exactly how the two items measure up, element by element. This is a more sophisticated way of organizing a comparison and contrast essay, as the following sample outlines demonstrate:

THE RELATIONSHIP BETWEEN CREATOR AND CREATED IN *PINOCCHIO* AND *FRANKENSTEIN*	
Point-by-Point Technique	**Simple Comparison and Contrast Technique**
A. Creating the monster 1. Pinocchio's creation 2. the creature's creation	A. Gepetto and Pinocchio 1. Pinocchio's creation 2. Geppetto's reaction 3. relationship between Pinocchio and Geppetto
B. The cost of creation 1. Geppetto's reaction 2. Frankenstein's reaction	B. Frankenstein and the creature 1. the creature's creation 2. Frankenstein's reaction 3. relationship between the creature and Frankenstein
C. Creator and created 1. relationship between Pinocchio and Geppetto 2. relationship between the creature and Frankenstein	

Practice 1

On a separate sheet of paper or on your computer, plan a response to the following assignment:

Assignment: Explore the different ways adolescence is presented in contemporary media (e.g., television and film, literature, online, etc.).

1. Identify your topic and compose a goal statement.
2. Use one of the brainstorming techniques from Lessons 3 and 4 to generate ideas.
3. Use the thesis templates from Lesson 5 to compose a tentative thesis.
4. Create an outline using classification or comparison and contrast as your organizing principle.

Cause and Effect

Another way to organize ideas is using cause and effect. This method works in either direction:

1. **cause → effect:** what happened (*cause*) and what happened as a result (*effect*)
2. **effect → cause:** what happened (*effect*) and why it happened (*cause*)

Like chronology, cause and effect can be an essay's main organizational structure, or it can be used to organize a specific section. It can also be used in combination with other organizing principles. For example, if your assignment was to discuss the events that led to World War I, you would probably use cause and effect as well as chronology to organize your ideas.

Here's part of an outline for an essay about the effects of the Industrial Revolution on city life.

    1. Industries moved to cities
        A. Large influx of working class from rural areas, looking for jobs
            1. Crowded, unsanitary conditions
            2. Children in the streets (unsupervised) or working in factories (uneducated)
            3. Demand for more hospitals, police, sanitation, social services

Problem → Solution

Like cause and effect, problem → solution essays connect two levels of analyses into one response. First, the writer must explain the scope of the problem, and then he or she must offer a well-argued solution that fully addresses that problem. Here is an effective organizational structure for a problem → solution portion of an essay:

I. Problem Analysis
   A. Classification/definition of the problem
   B. Cause of the problem
   C. Effect/extent of the problem
II. Solution Proposal
   A. Explanation of best solution to the problem and why it address the problem's effects
   B. Implications (what would occur if solution were implemented)
   C. Call to action/next steps

Notice how the **problem → solution** approach incorporates other organizational strategies, including cause and effect and classification. For example, if a student were evaluating a proposal to require all students at his high school to wear uniforms, he may choose to review what led to the proposal (e.g., inappropriate attire, student misbehavior) and the effect the problem or the proposed solution may have on the school. His solution may then advocate for or against uniforms or offer an alternative—for example, to set guidelines for what can be worn rather than setting a strict uniform code.

Practice 2

On a separate sheet of paper or your computer, plan a response to the following assignment:

Assignment: *Discuss a problem in your school or community you would like to see addressed. What is causing this problem, and what effect is it having on the school and/or community? Propose a solution, if applicable.*

1. Identify your topic and compose a goal statement.
2. Use one of the brainstorming techniques from Lessons 3 or 4 to generate ideas.
3. Use the thesis templates from Lesson 5 to compose a tentative thesis.
4. Create an outline using cause and effect or problem → solution as your organizing principle.

Summary

Classification, comparison and contrast, cause and effect, and problem → solution are four strategies to help organize your essay ideas. One strategy can serve as an overall organizing principle, while others may help you organize individual paragraphs and sections of your essay.

Skill Building Practice

Find an essay or article that utilizes multiple organizational strategies. Review the structure of the text carefully. What does the author do to integrate some of these strategies to help convey his/her perspective? How will the author's technique inform your own writing?

SECTION

SECTION

2 ▶

DRAFTING
THE ESSAY

N OW THAT YOU'VE done some planning, you're warmed up and ready to write. The lessons in this section will show you how to draft a successful essay, from introduction to conclusion. You'll learn how to support your ideas with evidence and details, and how to make arguments that are more convincing.

8 ▶ THE DRAFTING PROCESS

LESSON SUMMARY

In this lesson, you'll learn how to get started on a rough draft from your brainstorming notes. You'll also learn how to develop strong essay paragraphs.

What does writing an essay remind you of? Think for a minute what writing is like for you. Many students compare it to the creation of a whole new universe, built by words and ideas. You too can create a compelling essay universe by using some effective essay building strategies.

Where to Begin?

The planning steps in Section 1 of this book have enabled you to break down the assignment, brainstorm ideas, focus your topic, develop a tentative thesis, and design an outline, which are essential building blocks for a great essay. Now it's time for next steps. Get one of your outlines out, place your thesis at the top of the page, and try one of these techniques to get the drafting process under way.

Focused Brainstorm

This is a good time to return to the brainstorming activities in Lessons 3 and 4 (looping and cubing in particular), and to apply them to a specific paragraph or section. You can also try "exploding the moment" for a particular idea or paragraph in your paper: what sensory details (*see, think, feel, does, says*) are associated with the concept? If needed, consider returning to the thesis template in Lesson 5 to clarify a paragraph or section's main ideas, arguments, etc.

Apply Organizational Strategies

As discussed in Lessons 6 and 7, your essay outline should already be organized according to the organizational strategies you intend to use. If it's not, your first step is to sequence ideas so they reflect a chronology, comparison, causal analysis, etc.

Practice 1

Select one of the practice items you completed for Lesson 7 and use one of the three strategies suggested in this section to start drafting a response. See how much you can accomplish in 20 minutes.

Paragraphs

By definition, a **paragraph** is one or more sentences about a single idea. They're also one of a writer's most important tools. They divide the text into manageable pieces of information, and lead the reader by signaling the introduction of new ideas.

The following is an example of a complete paragraph. What common elements of a paragraph can you spot in it?

> *The African country of the Democratic Republic of Congo has had a turbulent past. It was colonized by Belgium in the late nineteenth century and officially declared a Belgian territory by King Leopold in 1895. The country, called the Belgian Congo after 1908, was under Belgian rule for 65 years. In 1960, after several years of unrest, Congo was granted independence from Belgium. The country was unstable for several years. Two presidents were elected and deposed, and there was much arguing over who should run the country and how. In 1965, a man named Mobutu Sese Seko rose to power. Though the country was remarkably rich in resources such as diamonds, under Sese Seko's rule, the people lived in complete squalor. Still, Sese Seko brought some stability to the region. He ruled for 32 years, until the people finally rebelled in 1997.*

The first sentence in the paragraph introduced the topic and expressed its main idea; it is the paragraph's topic sentence. The next seven sentences develop and support that idea. Then, the last two sentences conclude the paragraph. They remind readers of the main idea (the country's unstable past) and lead them into the next paragraph by introducing the 1997 rebellion that removed Sese Seko from power.

Paragraphs are not accidents. When composed effectively, they are deliberate, orderly, and clear. They are held together by one controlling idea. This idea is usually stated in a topic sentence and supported by the remaining sentences.

Practice 2

Divide the following text into paragraphs. Underline the topic sentence in each paragraph you create:

Sigmund Freud, the father of psychoanalysis, made many contributions to the science of psychology. One of his greatest contributions was his theory of the personality. According to Freud, the human personality is made up of three parts: the id, the ego, and the superego. The id is the part of the personality that exists only in the subconscious. According to Freud, the id has no direct contact with reality. It is the innermost core of our personality and operates according to the pleasure principle. That is, it seeks immediate gratification for its desires, regardless of external realities or consequences. It is not even aware that external realities or consequences exist. The ego develops from the id and is the part of the personality in contact with the real world. The ego is conscious and therefore aims to satisfy the subconscious desire of the id as best it can within the individual's environment. When it can't satisfy those desires, it tries to control or suppress the id. The ego functions according to the reality principle. The superego is the third and final part of the personality to develop. This part of the personality contains our moral values and ideals, our notion of what's right and wrong. The superego gives us the rules that help the ego control the id. For example, a child wants a toy that belongs to another child (id). He checks his environment to see if it's possible to take that toy (ego). He can, and does. Then he remembers that it's wrong to take something that belongs to someone else (superego), and returns the toy.

Developing Strong Paragraphs

What did you do when completing Practice 1 to separate the text in a logical sequence of paragraphs? Most likely, you looked for sentences that seemed to serve a particular role—as transitions, as different ideas, as evidence supporting previous statements. As you start drafting, it may be helpful to apply the same logic to your drafting: start first by determining the desired function of the sentence in the paragraph and consider, briefly, what idea you want to convey. Map out the *what* and *why* of the sentence(s), and you're ready to compose. Consider our earlier example on the Congo (the first example is done for you; fill in the spaces for the other two examples):

MAP	IDEA	SENTENCE
Function		
Introduce paragraph	History of instability	The African country of the Democratic Republic of Congo has had a turbulent past.
	Start with European colonization	It was colonized by Belgium in the late nineteenth century and officially declared a Belgian territory by King Leopold in 1895.
		The country, called the Belgian Congo after 1908, was under Belgian rule for 65 years.

Note how a graphic organizer like this comes in handy when collecting and organizing your thoughts. It allows us to get really granular, knowing the exact purpose and content of each sentence before composing. That helps a lot when you're just trying to get thoughts on paper.

It also helps to have a rich structure to follow, so that you know what the function of the sentence should be.

One possible method for analytical and argumentative essay assignments is what is known as Toulmin structure (named after the man who invented it), which was originally intended for legal scholars. That's the key advantage of the model: it's structured to encourage well-reasoned and well-supported thinking, the kind that builds paragraphs so they each convey a complete thought. Here is an example outline of this model:

1. **Topic sentence:** states the main idea of the paragraph
2. **Reason**(s): explains the causes or support for the main idea
3. **Evidence:** describes the data or proof for the main idea
4. **Backing:** explains how the evidence supports the main idea
5. **Qualifier/Rebuttal/Concession:** discusses when or how the main idea is true or not true in other situations (discussed in greater detail in Lesson 10)

This is not to suggest that a paragraph must be no more and no less than five sentences; it may be that your evidence or qualifier requires several sentences of explanation, or that a concession is not necessary. The structure is merely a guide to ensure your paragraphs have appropriate depth.

The example that follows comes from an SAT Writing task, which asks test takers whether understanding one's own identity requires him or her to turn inward. It has been reproduced as both a full paragraph and in the table, so that you can see how the components of the Toulmin work separately and together. Note that this writer included both a qualifier and rebuttal in his response.

Those with the most profound sense of understanding of life, or hold a strong self-identity, are those who chose not to follow the crowd. We cannot understand life ourselves simply by having the ideas and values of others thrust upon us; our ability to truly understand these features and to reshape them for our ends must be done internally. This is particularly evident when looking at the lives of important philosophers like Nietzsche and Socrates, each of whom came to grasp something essential about life by removing themselves from the city so they could think and write. By separating themselves from the masses, both philosophers were able to ponder what it means to be human without being influenced by surrounding human interests; this separation and turn inward enabled each to develop a clear worldview that would change how we view the world. Of course, the examples of two philosophical giants might suggest that very few people every truly understand themselves; however, given, the complexity of the world in which we live, that's not unexpected. Besides, how many people truly turn inward in a meaningful fashion? Millions of people are happy and confident without necessarily turning inward; however, I say these people are acting according to the social roles "scripted" for them rather than any internal calculus—this is not understanding the self.

TOULMIN STEPS	SENTENCE
Topic Sentence	Those with the most profound sense of understanding of life, or hold a strong self-identity, are those who chose not to follow the crowd.
Reasoning	We cannot understand life our ourselves simply by having the ideas and values of others thrust upon us; our ability to truly understand these features and to reshape them for our ends must be done internally.
Evidence	This is particularly evident when looking at the lives of important philosophers like Nietzsche and Socrates, each of whom came to grasp something essential about life by removing themselves from the city so they could think and write.
Backing	By separating themselves from the masses, both philosophers were able to ponder what it means to be human without being influenced by surrounding human interests; this separation and turn inward enabled each to develop a clear worldview that would change how we view the world.
Qualifier	Of course, the examples of two philosophical giants might suggest that very few people every truly understand themselves; however, given, the complexity of the world in which we live, that's not unexpected. Besides, how many people truly turn inward in a meaningful fashion?
Rebuttal	Millions of people are happy and confident without necessarily turning inward; however, I say these people are acting according to the social roles "scripted" for them rather than any internal calculus—this is not understanding the self.

Practice 3

Continue developing the response you started in Practice 1 for this lesson by developing the body paragraphs. Use the following paragraph map and/or the Toulmin model to organize your paragraph ideas and flow. Compose your response on another sheet of paper or a computer.

FUNCTION	IDEA	SENTENCE

In Short

Initial drafting of an essay is meant to be a continuation of the work completed during the planning stages. A paragraph is a group of sentences that are organized to fully and meaningfully express a single controlling idea. Identifying the function and idea of each sentence enables you to compose clearer and coherent sentences and paragraphs.

Skill Building Practice

Use one of the drafting techniques covered in this lesson the next time you begin an essay and reflect on the process. Which one did you choose, and why? How did the experience compare to your usual methods of beginning a draft? Would you use the strategy again? Why or why not?

9 ▶ PROVIDING SUPPORT

LESSON SUMMARY

Your essay evidence is as important as the thesis it supports. This lesson describes six different strategies for supporting your assertions.

An essay is an explanation, not just of what you think, but of why you think it. Readers want to see both deep subject knowledge and a unique viewpoint; it's not enough to simply provide a grocery list of your supporting reasons. Your *why* must comprise many types of support—including evidence, examples, and details—that are knowledgeably and meaningfully articulated in your writing. Six kinds of support this lesson covers are:

1. reasons
2. facts
3. specific examples
4. descriptions and anecdotes
5. expert opinions and analysis
6. quotations from the text

The boundaries of these categories are not absolute; an anecdote is often an example, and a reason can also be a fact. However, the categories are useful for discussing types of support and illustrating how to substantiate your assertions in a variety of ways.

Reasons

For many essays, the best way to support the thesis is to explain why you think the way you do. In the Toulmin model introduced in Lesson 8, those reasons immediately follow a topic sentence, in order to provide logical grounds for believing what you do. Think of reasons as completing the following statement:

My thesis/topic sentence is true because _____.

Consider the following thesis, one quite typical of a high school writer:

School officials should not be allowed to randomly search students' lockers and backpacks.

For support, the following reasons could be used:

- these searches violate the right to privacy
- searches should not be done randomly, but only when there is a suspected violation

As you can see, reasons are the thinking behind the main idea; however, they are not always evidence in and of themselves—they need to be based on evidence or good common sense. That is, they must be logical. They can't simply be stated with an expectation that the audience will believe them.

Both of the previous reasons, for example, are opinions, and they need support to be convincing. To support the first reason, the writer could define the right to privacy (a combination of specific examples, facts, and description). He could provide an example or describe a certain situation where a search led to a violation of privacy (specific example, anecdote); and provide an expert opinion.

To support the second assertion, he could explore the idea that random searches can lead to profiling of who is searched and, without a suspected violation, everyone then becomes a suspect unless otherwise cleared of a violation. He could then provide expert opinion.

Facts

Ask any young writer what good evidence is and you'll likely get a one-word answer: facts. If it's true—or at least appears like it could be true—it must be good, right? Many ACT and SAT test takers will generate facts on the writing portions of these tests, under the presumption that such data inevitably impresses. Unfortunately, their fake facts are often as absurd as you can imagine.

Facts must be handled diligently—they are a means, not an end. In elementary or middle school, your teacher may have praised you for collecting three or more statistics just because it showed you did some research; in high school and college, your teachers are looking beyond whether your statistics, definitions, and observations are right or not. They want to know that you've considered the context of the fact, understand its application, and know its power and limitations.

A gaudy statistic can be impressive, no doubt, but advanced writers think about how facts fit into the entirety of their arguments, not just whether it flatters their egos. A fact is only as useful as what the writer does with it.

Suppose a writer is drafting an essay assessing the flat tax. She's gathered the following facts to support her thesis (*A flat tax would be good for the government and for citizens*):

- The IRS publishes 480 different tax forms.
- The IRS publishes 280 different tax forms to explain those 480 tax forms.
- The body of the tax law has 7.05 million words—ten times the number of words in the Bible.
- The cost of income tax compliance is over $1.3 billion a year (some sources estimate the cost as high as $2 billion).

How would you utilize these statistics in an essay on the flat tax? Sure, 480 tax forms sounds like several hundred too many—but what is the direct connection between the number of forms and the stance of the thesis, that a flat tax would offer a better way? After asking questions about relevance, not all of these statistics may be useful to the writer's argument.

Practice 1

Choose one of the essays for which you developed an outline in Lesson 6 or 7. Identify the reasons supporting your thesis, and for each describe one fact and one specific example that backs up your reasoning. Use the Toulmin model from Lesson 8 to compose at least one paragraph that incorporates your reasons and evidence.

Description and Anecdotes

Evidence and support can also come in the form of short stories or descriptions that illustrate a point. Descriptions and anecdotes are effective evidence—especially in essays about people—because they help the reader form a picture that illuminates your ideas. In the following thesis, the writer addresses a college application essay topic:

The person I admire most is my sister. I call her Wonder Woman. A professional who copes daily with the most stressful and potentially depressing situations, she is the strongest person I know.

The best kind of support for this essay will likely be descriptions and anecdotes—a series of snapshots and stories that illustrate the sister's strength. Here's an example:

Amy's job with the Division of Youth and Family Services is incredibly stressful. Every day for the past five years, she has visited families who are struggling with addiction, abuse, poverty, and hopelessness. One family has been in the system for a decade, cycling through the same problems without resolution. But instead of burning out, Amy's compassion and resolve have increased. She visits this family weekly, and is available to them almost 24 hours a day should a crisis arise. Once, she was awakened at three in the morning when the teenager in this family failed to come home. She got in her car and drove to their apartment, and then called the police and helped them file a missing persons report. And this is just one family under her watch.

Similarly, to support the assertion that searches of students' lockers and backpacks should not be allowed, you could describe a search in which a student was unfairly accused of and blamed for a crime. The following description appeared in a law journal article about such as case:

Wearing an orange prison jumpsuit and flip-flops, Sam Mazza looked dejected as he made his first court appearance. He was facing three years in prison for a crime he says was intended as a private joke. His spirits appeared to lift, however, when his attorney carefully laid out his case: The search of every locker in the school was unconstitutional. When Mazza's principal ordered the search, he was in violation of the reasonable suspicion component of legal searches.

Since the note about a bomb threat (Mazza contends it was a joke) was found during an illegal search, the case had to be dropped. Mazza sat taller in his seat and smiled at his parents when his attorney concluded his remarks.

Expert Opinion and Analysis

During a trial, lawyers often call upon expert witnesses to help them make their cases. These witnesses were not involved in the crime, but they have expertise that can help the jurors determine the guilt or innocence of the defendant. Similarly, in many essays, and particularly in research papers, much of your support will come in the form of expert opinion and analysis—from credible subject matter experts in the field who can help you demonstrate the validity of your thesis. This expertise is derived from Internet, periodicals, journals, books, and transcripts.

The strength of expert opinion and analysis as evidence comes from the fact that your sources are experts. Think about the groups of people whose opinion on your topic would add credibility to your argument—and those who would not. Take, for instance, the flat tax topic presented earlier. An accountant in your community, for instance, surely has an opinion on the topic—but is he an expert on it? He or she is certainly less of an expert than an economics professor or a politician who is a proponent or opponent of a flat tax. Support for a flat tax could be asserted using the following expert sources:

The Tax Foundation, a nonprofit tax think tank, estimates that America spends $140 billion complying with the current tax code—a cost that would be reduced 94% by instituting a flat tax.

Expert analysis is more challenging to utilize, but is no less useful on timed writing exams. You will not be able to directly quote an expert or reference their knowledge, but you can talk about how a group of people is likely to respond to a topic, and provide examples or descriptions that enable you to speak for them.

For instance, if the task were to argue for or against school uniforms, it is well within your power to consider how teachers, administrators, parents, and even the community would respond to the new clothing requirements. How would these constituents be affected by such a change in policy? What would their opinion be on the issue?

Quotations from a Text

When your essay is about a specific piece of literature, much of your evidence will come from the text itself. For example, imagine that you've written the following thesis statement:

In his poem "Splinter," Carl Sandburg uses metaphor and sound to suggest loss.

To support your assertion, you will need to discuss the poem's content, structure, and style. But that's only part of the task. In addition to telling the reader why you think what you do about the poem, you also need to show them the evidence that led to your conclusion. You can tell readers that the poem suggests loss by the repetition of the short *i* sound (known as a phonetic intensive in line 4 (*thin, splinter, singing*). You can also explain how metaphor is used to emphasize the same theme, and show evidence by quoting the last line, which describes the voice of the last cricket by comparing it to a thin splinter:

The voice of the last cricket
across the first frost
is one kind of good-by.
It is so thin a splinter of singing.

Practice 2

Provide support for another essay outlined in Lesson 6 or 7, or add more support to the essay you used for Practice 1 in this lesson. Identify the reasons supporting your thesis, and for each provide one description or anecdote, expert opinion and analysis, and quotation from the text. Use the Toulmin model from Lesson 8 to compose at least one paragraph that incorporates your reasons and evidence.

Summary

Evidence enables writers to demonstrate more than a position, including how and why they think the way they do. Evidence supports the writer's reasoning and comes in the form of facts, specific examples, descriptions and anecdotes, expert opinion and analysis, and quotations from the text.

Skill Building Practice

Read an opinion piece on the editorial page of a newspaper or website. How does the author support his or her ideas? What kind of evidence does he or she provide? After you read the piece, keep it handy because you'll need to use it again in Lesson 11.

10 ▶ STRATEGIES FOR CONVINCING

LESSON SUMMARY

This lesson offers several strategies to help increase the depth and persuasiveness of your writing.

The first descriptive line for earning the top score on the Writing portion of the ACT states that to get a 6, one must "address complexity by offering a critical context for discussion, examining different perspectives on the issue, evaluating the implications and/or complications of the issue, or by fully responding to counterarguments to the writer's position."

What does it mean to "address complexity," exactly? Complexity is an intangible element that separates effective writers from the rest. Evidence counts, of course, but equally as important is the depth of conversation about that evidence—the connections you can make, the awareness you show, the intellectual quality of your ideas. Ultimately, your evaluators are determining if can you demonstrate your most thoughtful thinking on the subject provided. Here are four strategies that work with your supporting evidence to make your essays more thoughtful and convincing:

1. Addressing context
2. Qualifying your position
3. Acknowledging counterarguments.
4. Making connections

Addressing Context

Ideas don't exist in a vacuum, and neither do essay assignments. They may arise from a text, a national or local issue, or even from you and your classmates' interests and concerns. Your evaluator's primary purpose in assigning the task is to promote your thinking and understanding. For example, to understand what brought upon the Civil War, a historian's viewpoint would be informed by multiple contexts: the major events leading up to disunion (historical); the ways in which people of different classes and races interacted (social); the economies of the North versus the South (economic)—each would enable the writer to make deep connections between what is known about the topic and his or her own perspective on the issues. When writing an essay, your ability to situate your position in the ongoing discussion of your topic is essential.

The following are three readily available context types with which you are likely already familiar. The key is to incorporate them into your writing intentionally.

Historical Precedent

Alluding to historical situations or persons can convey the significance of your position, or the source of your ideas. By connecting your position to important facets of history, you can draw out a rich and important context for why your position is credible. For example, if asked to assess the concept of teaching boys and girls separately, one could critique single-gender classrooms by discussing the women's suffrage movement, with the writer noting that separating genders now would create a climate that was *not* equal.

Note that merely identifying the suffrage moment, or any historical event alone, is meaningless without the critical thinking component. Your example must be relevant to the task, logically explained, and connect to your position.

Norms

Discussing common behaviors, attitudes, beliefs, and practices can provide insight into the motives of the subject matter or those involved with it. Such traits are called norms because they represent what is normal in relation to your essay. This can be a group of people, but it can also refer to events, situations, and behaviors.

For example, the student who earlier supported rewards for high test scores may make the case that "American society values the ideals of hard work, sacrifice, responsibility, and the idea that, if one demonstrates these traits, they are rewarded." Here, the writer has involved "American values" to make his case, thereby connecting with a set of ideals and beliefs that not only explains why some might support giving money to students for doing well on a test, but also connects with readers on an emotional level.

Contemporary Relevance

By discussing the reasons why your topic matters in contemporary society you can address many of the most important issues, conflicts, and values of today's world. For example, writing about students receiving rewards for strong performance on tests or schoolwork addresses the current national policy debate on testing, the disparities in student achievement among various demographics, and the purpose of education in general. Imagine how much you could write about if you addressed whether high test scores are an essential part of educational success!

Practice 1

With the essay topic you have been developing since Lesson 6, address context by brainstorming responses to the following questions:

How has your topic developed historically? How does it compare to other similar or different concepts?

_____

_____

_____

_____

_____

What issues exist today that indicate the importance of this topic?

_____

_____

_____

_____

_____

What common beliefs, attitudes, and behaviors are associated with the topic? Why?

_____

_____

_____

_____

_____

Review your responses and your plans for your essay. Where and how could you embed these ideas into a draft on the topic?

_____

_____

_____

_____

_____

Qualifying your position

When writing persuasively, it's easy to fall into the trap of thinking in terms of black and white—that there are only two sides to an issue, and that one side must be wrong. The remedy is *qualification*—the specification of what conditions or circumstances are necessary for a position to be true or false. For example, if you were asked to discuss whether physical education should be mandatory, you might write:

"Physical education coursework should only be mandatory for freshmen and sophomores."

Notice how the thesis statement narrows the application of the position to a specific group of people (*freshmen and sophomores*). Such a position expands the reach of the argument; you could not only argue why gym is important for underclassmen, you might also find it relevant to discuss what coursework upperclassmen need and why gym is not essential as you move closer to graduation. Specifying the grounds for your position actually provides *more* ideas for discussion than a this-or-that-side approach, not to mention offering greater clarity to your readers. All it takes is asking and answering two questions:

- **Who is or isn't affected by my position?**
- **In what situations is that effect evident?**

In the Toulmin model (presented in Lesson 8), a qualification statement comes after the writer explains how the evidence supports the topic sentence and reasons. Here, a writer may choose to acknowledge those cases where the support may not be true, or he/she may need to set the conditions for the topic sentence to be true. The following sentence starters can assist you when composing qualification statements:

If _____, then _____.
_____, but only if _____.
When _____, then it follows that _____.
For _____, it is likely that _____.

Addressing Counterarguments

An important part of establishing your credibility and persuading readers is demonstrating an understanding of how others may view your topic, and the effect these viewpoints have on your position. There are three ways of addressing counterarguments:

- acknowledging different perspectives
- concession
- rebuttal

Acknowledging different perspectives may refer to explaining the traits of an opposing argument, an alternative position or stance, or even similar positions to your own. Doing so shows that you have considered all sides of the issue and thought carefully about the logic of your position and those of others: What is commonly believed and/or felt about this topic? Why? What common ground is there? Is there any division? You may choose to follow this discussion by identifying the strengths of such perspectives, or choose to explain why your stance remains superior to others.

A **concession** is an acknowledgement that some aspect or position of a counterargument to your stance is valid or correct, but that such a truth is alone not persuasive enough to change the writer's position. For example, a writer who believes physical education should not be mandatory for high school upperclassmen may acknowledge that the opposing side is right to worry about the risks of increased obesity and bad health decisions that may result from eliminating gym; however, the greatest need of upperclassmen in the writer's school, she asserts, is time and guidance—the high risk of dropping out of college is more pressing than potential weight gain, she argues.

A **rebuttal** is the refutation of counterarguments to your stance by addressing objections to your position and explaining why they are erroneous or overstated. Here, you take the offensive—you recognize what objections your readers might have, and you can systematically address those objections in your essay (without, in many cases, revealing them as possible objections).

For example, the supporter of the flat tax might get a jump on opponents who'd criticize the decrease in tax revenues from the rich by noting how the flat tax would remove loopholes that currently enable wealthier taxpayers to pay significantly less than they should.

To help you acknowledge counterarguments, play devil's advocate. While brainstorming or outlining, take a few minutes to consider the opposite thesis. How would it best be supported? What arguments would likely be made? If you can anticipate what the other side will say, you can acknowledge those arguments and come up with effective counterarguments. It will also help you find any holes in your argument that you may have missed.

Practice 2

You are writing an essay on the subject of censorship on the Internet. Take a stance on this issue and write a brief thesis statement on a separate sheet of paper or on your computer. Come up with three supporting points. Next, play devil's advocate and list three points the opposition might make. Finally, write a brief paragraph in which you acknowledge one of those points.

Practice 3

Revise one of the paragraphs you developed in Lesson 8 or 9 using the Toulmin model, so that the paragraph contains a qualification and a concession or rebuttal.

Making Connections

If context enables us to see prior events, and beliefs inform current understanding of an essay topic, then the two strategies detailed in this section, **evaluating implications** and **addressing underlying values**, help us project how the topic might work in the future. This forecasting of how your position or proposal may function in the real world gives readers a clear sense of the weight and value of your stance.

Evaluating Implications

To evaluate implications is to analyze what would result if an action—say, giving students money for scoring well on an important test—were to occur. For example, consider what often happens after a sharp rise in gas prices: less oil is consumed and more people take public transportation—these are implications, or consequences, of the price increase.

In other words, you are assessing the impact of an event or action on those connected to it. Do positive or negative changes arise as a result of your position? One negative implication of giving students money for high test scores, for instance, is that those students may not want to continue working hard in school if material rewards are not continually provided to them for their efforts.

Note the word evaluating in this approach, for it requires the writer to provide two components to the reader:

1. A description of what is likely to result if the position of the essay is true or takes place (e.g., what happens if you are accepted into the school to which you are applying).
2. A judgment on whether the results are worthwhile (e.g., the long-term advantage to the school for having you as a student).

In analyzing and evaluating this way, you convey an understanding of both short-term issues and long-term outcomes.

Underlying Values

Debates exist because people invariably have conflicting values or principles regarding a topic. You have your values and principles too, ones that subtly and not-so subtly inform your position. Think about how and why these beliefs led to your position, and how they might conflict with other values and viewpoints. Why is this topic or issue difficult to resolve? Identification of the ideological conflict(s) behind the various perspectives on an issue helps you to highlight the significance of the topic.

Practice 4

Select one of the essay topics you have been developing over the course of the last several lessons. Create supporting paragraphs for your thesis that support the main idea by developing claims involving at least two of the following: addressing context, discussing qualifiers, acknowledging counter-arguments, evaluating implications, and/or analyzing underlying values.

Summary

Writers use many strategies to make their essays more convincing. They address context, qualify their positions, acknowledge counterarguments, and draw connections between their ideas and the real world applications of those ideas.

Skill Building Practice

Look at the Skill Building Practice essay you read in the previous lesson. What strategies for convincing do you see at work? In what ways is using these strategies effective or ineffective?

11 ▶ INTRODUCTIONS

LESSON SUMMARY

First impressions are important. This lesson explains the purpose of introductions, and how to write a hook that grabs a reader's attention.

Right or wrong, many decisions in life are based solely on first impressions. In the business world, for instance, companies spend millions of dollars on advertising to make sure your first impression of them is a good one. First impressions are just as important in writing. It is unlikely that a college admissions officer who's reading his 40th essay of the day will be moved by a response that begins, "In this essay, I will . . ." The introduction is a critical part of any essay, and if it's not fully developed it can diminish what might otherwise be a well-written piece.

What an Introduction Should Do

The introduction sells the essay to the reader and acquaints the audience with the subject and purpose of the essay. An effective introduction should do the following:

- **Provide the context necessary to understand your thesis.** When you're writing for a general audience, your readers don't know who you are. They may not know your assignment and may not be familiar with the issues or texts you are discussing. You might need to provide background information, such as titles, authors, and publication dates of the text(s) you are analyzing. Here's an example:

> Mary Shelley's novel Frankenstein was published over 180 years ago. But this remarkable novel raises a question that is more important today than ever: What is a creator's responsibility for his or her creation?

- **Clearly state the main point of the essay.** Your readers should know from the beginning what idea(s) you will be developing throughout your essay. A clear thesis statement is a key component of an effective introduction (see Lesson 5 for a review of thesis statements). In the previous example, the last sentence expresses the main idea of the essay—the question, and its relevance today.

- **Hook the reader.** The introduction should not only get the reader's attention, but compel him or her to keep reading. The next section examines some of the many ways to write a successful hook. Consider the following:

> I will never forget the moment I landed in Rio de Janeiro. As the plane descended, I was awed by the dynamic geography and the juxtaposition of the sea, the mountains, and the city's skyline. I absorbed the landscape further and my eyes focused on the favelas mounted on the hillsides.

This introduction works well on a number of levels: It takes the reader to an exotic location, describes the landscape, and sets the scene. The writer tells you that the moment is unforgettable, and brings you along with her.

- **Set the tone for the essay.** Tone refers to the attitude of the writer towards his/her subject matter as conveyed through language, particularly through word choice and sentence structure. Your tone may be personal and informal, serious and formal, urgent, relaxed, grave, or humorous. In the *Frankenstein* example, the language is serious and formal, and it fits the serious subject (supporting examples in the essay may include discussions of atomic weapons and cloning).

Hook Your Reader

A good hook contains an element of creativity and an awareness of the reader's needs. It doesn't simply announce the subject or thesis, or make generalizations that sound cliché. Phrases such as *one step at a time, no news is good news, have a nice day*, and *no guts, no glory* are so overused they have little or no meaning.

The following six introductory hook strategies offer specific and effective ways to get into your subject and thesis:

1. a quotation
2. a question
3. a surprising statement or fact
4. an imaginary situation or scenario
5. an anecdote
6. a new twist on a familiar phrase

A Quotation

Start with a quote from a text, a film, a subject-matter expert, or even a friend or relative if he or she said something relevant to the topic. Here's an example:

> "All animals are equal, but some animals are more equal than others," said Napoleon in George Orwell's classic novel Animal Farm. Uncle Sam might say something similar: "All people must pay taxes, but some must pay more taxes than others." Our current federal income tax system treats taxpayers unfairly and requires a monumental budget to administer and maintain. A flat tax, which would treat all taxpayers equally and dramatically reduce tax compliance costs, is the answer.

A Question

Open up with a question to get your readers thinking. Of course, the question (and its answer) should be relevant to your thesis. Consider the following:

> What's in a name? Nothing—and everything. It is, after all, just a name, one tiny piece of the puzzle that makes up a person. But when someone has a nickname like Dumbo, a name can be a major force in shaping one's sense of self. That's how it was for me.

A Surprising Statement or Fact

This type of hook can provide shock value for the reader, as in the following example:

> If you don't believe our current tax law is ridiculously out of control, consider this: Our tax law consists of 101,295 pages and 7.05 million words. That means our tax law has almost 100 times more pages and ten times as many words as the Bible. Bloated? You bet. But it doesn't have to be. The government would collect equal or greater tax revenue and save millions of dollars in compliance costs by instituting a flat tax system.

Practice 1

On a separate sheet of paper or on your computer, use a quotation, a question, or a surprising statement or fact to write two introductory hooks for one of the essays you brainstormed or outlined in an earlier lesson. When you're finished, identify which of the two hooks best fits the purpose and content of the assignment.

An Imaginary Situation or Scenario

Hook your readers using your imagination. You might ask them to place themselves in the scene, or you can let them simply witness it. Here's an example:

> You've been drifting at sea for days with no food and no water. You have two companions. Suddenly, a half-empty bottle of water floats by. You fight over the bottle, ready to kill the others if you have to for that water. What has happened? What are you—human or animal? It is a question that H.G. Wells raised over and over in "The Island of Dr.Moreau." His answer? Like it or not, we're both.

An Anecdote

Start your essay by telling a short, interesting story related to your subject, as follows:

> I'd been getting into a lot of trouble—failing classes, taking things that didn't belong to me. The guidance counselor at school suggested that my parents take me to a psychiatrist. "You mean a shrink?" my mother replied, horrified. My father and I had the same reaction. After all, what good would it do to lie on a couch while some doctor asked questions and took notes? I went to my first session angry and skeptical. But after a few weeks, I realized that we had it all wrong. Those shrinks really know what they're doing. And mine helped me turn my life around.

A New Twist on a Familiar Phrase

Reword or rework an old standard to create a fresh hook:

> To eat or not to eat? That is the question millions of Americans struggle with every day as they fight the battle of the bulge. But it seems to be a losing battle. Despite the millions of dollars spent on diet pills and diet plans, Americans today are heavier than ever.
>
> There are many reasons for this nationwide weight gain, but experts agree that the main cause is lack of exercise. And one of the reasons we don't get enough exercise is because we spend too much time in front of the TV.

Notice that this introduction is actually two paragraphs. In some essays, the introduction runs three or even four paragraphs. The key is to have an introduction that is in proportion with the rest of the essay. If your essay is two pages long, one paragraph is probably sufficient for the introduction. If it goes longer, the body of your essay (where you develop your main points and support them with evidence and examples) will lack the room it needs to completely state your case. But if your essay is ten or twelve pages long, it may take a couple of paragraphs to properly introduce your topic and thesis. You might have a more detailed anecdote, for example, or spend two or three paragraphs describing a scenario that sets up your thesis.

Practice 2

Write a two-paragraph introduction for one of the essays you have been developing since Lesson 6 or 7. Use one of these strategies: an imaginary situation or scenario, an anecdote, or a new twist on a familiar phrase.

Summary

Introductions serve an important function. They welcome your reader into your essay by providing context, stating your thesis, and setting the tone. They should also grab your reader's interest. Strategies for attention-grabbing hooks include starting with a quotation, a question, a surprising statement or fact, an imaginary situation or scenario, an anecdote, or a new twist on a familiar phrase.

Skill Building Practice

Skim through a magazine, reading only the introductions to the articles. What techniques do writers use to grab your interest? Do the introductions provide context and state the main point of the articles? What tone do they set for the rest of the articles?

LESSON

12 ▶ CONCLUSIONS

LESSON SUMMARY

How you conclude your essay is just as important as how you introduce it. This lesson will explain what conclusions should do and how to write an ending that has impact.

Have you ever enjoyed a movie only to be disappointed by its ending? Although the ending may be just a small fraction of the movie's length, if it's not satisfying, it can ruin the whole experience. The same is often true for essays. A powerful conclusion can dramatically improve a reader's impression of a weak or mediocre essay, while a weak conclusion can do the reverse—leaving a bad impression of an otherwise well-written essay.

What a Conclusion Should Do

Like the introduction, the conclusion of an essay serves a specific function. Its job is to wrap things up in a way that makes readers feel satisfied with their reading experience. Writers create this sense of satisfaction by:

- restating the thesis in different words.
- offering a new understanding.
- providing a sense of closure.
- arousing the reader's emotions.

Restating the Thesis

Before your reader finishes your essay, remind him or her of what your goals are. What did you want him or her to take away from your essay? Reminding readers of your thesis (without repeating it word for word) will help ensure that they get your point. Consider the following introduction:

> What's in a name? Nothing—and everything. It is, after all, just a name, one tiny piece of the puzzle that makes up a person. But when someone has a nickname like Dumbo, a name can be the major force in shaping one's sense of self. That's how it was for me.

Now let's take a look at a possible conclusion:

> I don't blame my brother for how I turned out, of course. He may have given me the nickname, but I'm the one who let that nickname determine how I felt about myself. I could have worn the name proudly—after all, Disney's Dumbo is a hero. Instead, I wore it like a dunce cap. I wish I had known then what I know now: You are who you believe yourself to be.

Providing a Sense of Closure

Good conclusions often offer a new understanding, but that new understanding should be closely related to the thesis. The conclusion is not the time to introduce a new topic. Don't bring up assertions that have not already been supported by the body of your essay. Doing so will not only frustrate your reader, but will probably cause him or her to lose sight of your thesis. In the following examples, one conclusion provides closure while offering new understanding, while the other one goes off on a tangent unrelated to the original thesis:

> I don't blame my brother for how I turned out, of course. He may have given me the nickname, but I'm the one who let that nickname determine how I felt about myself. I could have worn the name proudly—after all, Disney's Dumbo is a hero. Instead, I wore it like a dunce cap. I wish I had known then what I know now: You are who you believe yourself to be.

Versus:

> I don't blame my brother for how I turned out, of course. He may have given me the nickname, but I'm the one who let that nickname determine how I felt about myself. I could have worn the name proudly—after all, Disney's Dumbo is a hero. Disney knew what he was doing when he created the Dumbo character—he's someone most of us can relate to, and he has a lot to teach children.

Even without reading the body of the essay, it is evident that the last sentence of the second conclusion doesn't relate closely to the thesis. The writer leaves his reader with thoughts about a movie and its creator, and not about his nickname and how it affected his sense of self. The first conclusion is more successful because it maintains close ties with the thesis, even as it draws a new conclusion and gives a new understanding about that thesis.

Arousing the Reader's Emotions

Good conclusions can also move readers by appealing to their emotions. Because your conclusion restates and extends your thesis by offering a new understanding, and because you want your essay to end with impact, it makes sense to write a memorable ending. One of the best ways to do that is through emotion. The conclusion to the *Dumbo* essay, for example, touches our emotions by making us think about how we may have let negative beliefs about ourselves dictate who we have become. At the same time, it inspires us by suggesting that we have the power to change ourselves if we have a negative self-image.

The Art of Framing

One of the most effective ways to provide a sense of closure is to frame your essay with a conclusion that refers to the introduction. The conclusion then serves as a reminder of where the essay began.

In the sample conclusions offered later in this lesson, notice how the conclusion frames the *Dumbo* essay by repeating the opening question and providing a more sophisticated answer. Similarly, the call to action conclusion frames the *To eat or not to eat?* essay by referring to the essay's opening lines.

Practice 1

Review the conclusions you composed for recent essay assignments for school against the criteria for good conclusions discussed in this section. Do your conclusions:

- reiterate your main idea?
- provide a sense of closure?
- connect with reader's emotions?
- refer back to or extend the introduction (framing)?

Which of these traits is evident in your earlier writing, and which is lacking? How does this relate to your usual approach to writing the final paragraph of an essay?

Strategies for Conclusions

Just as there are many strategies for creating an attention-getting introduction, there are a number of strategies for creating a powerful conclusion. These are among the most effective:

- a question
- an anecdote
- a prediction
- a solution or recommendation
- a call to action

You may have noticed that three of the introduction strategies we discussed in the previous lesson—quotations, questions, and anecdotes—are also effective for conclusions.

A Question

Here's how you might use a question to conclude an essay:

What kind of place is America? In short, America is an idea and an experiment. We call the idea democracy, and we see what happens when we let people say whatever they want, go wherever they want, and in most cases, do whatever they want. True, the results aren't always pretty. But it certainly is a beautiful experiment, isn't it?

An Anecdote

Anecdotes add interest and impact to conclusions. Notice how this anecdote frames the essay by repeating the question used in this introduction:

Introduction: What's in a name? Nothing—and everything. It is, after all, just a name, one tiny piece of the puzzle that makes up a person. But when someone has a nickname like Dumbo, a name can be the major force in shaping one's sense of self. That's how it was for me.

Conclusion: What's in a name? Enough to make me think long and hard about what to name my son. I spent months researching names and their meanings, and thinking about the nicknames people might come up with. Once we finally settled on a name, I spent many sleepless nights worrying that we'd made the wrong choice and petrified that Samuel James would hate us for giving him that name. But I've realized that along the way, Sam will have to learn the same life lessons I did. I only hope that I can help make them as painless as possible.

Practice 2

On a separate sheet of paper or on your computer, write a conclusion for an introduction you wrote in Lesson 11, using a question or an anecdote to frame the essay.

A Prediction

You can close your essay with a forecast for a person, place, or thing related to your thesis. Here's an example from a college application essay:

Thirty years from now, when I'm 48, I will retire and survey my empire. I will have created and led a hugely successful Fortune 500 company; I will have used my considerable wealth to set up a literacy foundation and a home for orphans in my native Cuba. Deeply satisfied with my accomplishments, I will then establish scholarships for disadvantaged students to Briarwood College, for I will recall with great gratitude that my education there made all of my accomplishments possible.

A Solution or Recommendation

Conclude with a solution to the problem(s) you've discussed, or a recommendation for future action. This strategy will serve you well later, when you're asked to write business memos or reports. Here is a conclusion from an essay that examines misinformation on the Internet:

> While the Internet can be a very valuable source of information, it contains so much misinformation that it's almost criminal. Although we can't—and shouldn't—regulate what people put up on the web, we can—and should—provide guidelines. Why not create a reliability index that measures the trustworthiness of websites? Then the Internet can truly be what it was meant to be: an asset, and not a liability.

A Call to Action

Finally, you can end your essay by suggesting a specific action that your readers should take. As with the solution or recommendation strategy, this one is also used often in business writing. Here's an example of a conclusion for an essay about television and lack of exercise. Notice how it frames the essay by referring to the opening line of the introduction.

> **Introduction:** To eat or not to eat? That is the question millions of Americans struggle with every day as they fight the battle of the bulge. But it seems to be a losing battle. Despite the millions spent on diet pills and diet plans, Americans today are heavier than ever. There are many reasons for this nationwide weight gain, but experts agree that the main cause is lack of exercise. And one of the reasons we don't get enough exercise is because we spend too much time in front of the TV.

> **Conclusion:** Television entertains and informs us. But it also fattens us. If you are one of the millions of overweight Americans, take a simple step toward a healthier body. Get up and turn off the TV. The question isn't "To eat or not to eat?" Rather, the question is, what can you do instead of watching TV? Go for a walk. Take a swim. Ride a bike. Get some exercise! You'll end up with a healthier body—and mind.

Practice 3

On a separate sheet of paper or on your computer, write a conclusion for an introduction you wrote for Lesson 11. Use one of the following strategies: a prediction, solution or recommendation, or call to action.

Summary

Like introductions, conclusions serve several important functions. They refocus the essay by restating the thesis; they offer a gift to the reader in the form of a new understanding (which is an extension of the thesis); they provide a sense of closure; and they arouse readers' emotions. Some of the same strategies for introductions also work for conclusions, including quotations, questions, and anecdotes. Other closing techniques include predictions, solutions or recommendations, and calls to action.

Skill Building Practice

Skim through a magazine, but this time, read the introductions and conclusions to at least three articles. What techniques do writers use to conclude their articles? Do the conclusions restate the main idea or thesis offered in the introduction? Do they go a step further and offer a new understanding? Do they provide a sense of closure? Do they speak to your emotions? What techniques do writers use to conclude their articles?

3 ▶ REVISING, EDITING, AND PROOFREADING THE ESSAY

O nce you have a rough draft of your essay, you are ready to transform it into a polished piece of writing. This polishing process consists of three steps: **revising, editing,** and **proofreading**. Think of them as holding up various strengths of magnifying glasses to your essay:

- **Revising** focuses on the essay as a whole, attending to the largest issues involved in its crafting—development, organization, etc. Have you addressed the topic? Is there a logical flow to your ideas or story? Is each paragraph necessary and properly placed?
- **Editing** takes a closer look at your writing, focusing on words and sentences. Are your word choices appropriate and fresh? Are there any repetitive or awkward sentences or phrases?
- **Proofreading** puts the focus at the word level: you will check *within* each word for errors in spelling and correct any other mechanical mistakes, such as grammar and punctuation.

13▶ REVISING: THE BIG PICTURE

LESSON SUMMARY

This is the first of two lessons dealing with the revision process. It shows you how to revise for three important big picture issues: fulfilling the assignment, stating a clear thesis, and providing strong support.

Revising and editing are not synonyms. Sure, it's common for students and even teachers to use the two words interchangeably, to describe the stage of writing after a draft has been written but before it is submitted for evaluation, but revision is much more than merely editing for correctness. It is a critical self-evaluation of your progress towards the goal(s) you or the assignment has established, and a significant opportunity to adjust and improve your writing.

Revision takes place at the big picture or essay level, as well as at the paragraph/sentence/word levels. It makes sense to look at your writing on these levels first, before jumping into editing or proofreading. Think of it this way—why take the time to correct grammatical errors and reword sentences if you might delete those sentences later in the revision process?

Revisioning

You can look at your essay with fresh eyes in two ways:

- giving your work to a trusted reader for feedback
- examining your own work as if you've never seen it before

If you think professional writers work alone, think again. They know how important it is to get feedback before they send their finished work. It's not uncommon for them to share their work with a number of trusted readers along the way. This strategy is important for your essays, too. Outside readers offer a fresh perspective, and can help you pinpoint the strengths and weaknesses of your writing. They can tell you what works well, and what doesn't; what comes across clearly to them, and what confuses them.

When you share your writing with people you trust to give you honest feedback, ask them:

- What do you like about my essay?
- Is there anything that seems confusing or unclear?
- What do you think my purpose was in writing this essay?
- Is there anything you need to know more about, or that needs more explanation?
- What do you think I could do to improve this essay?

These questions can also work when you direct them to yourself. However, before you reread your essay for revising, take a break. The best revisions take place a day or two after you've completed your draft. That time lets you approach your work fresh.

Try reading your essay aloud, as if you are presenting it to an audience. This technique can help you find places where your wording sounds awkward, or where your sentences are confusing or too long. You can also hear where your writing simply doesn't convey what you intended it to. Mark those areas that sound as if they should be revised, making notes of ideas for how to improve them. Remember to keep in mind the following:

- Does my essay fulfill the assignment?
- Is my thesis statement clear? Is it easily identifiable?
- Are my ideas well supported with examples, evidence, and details?

Reworking

Once you've received feedback and have taken your own notes on what could be improved, it's time to make changes. Those changes could be additions, deletions, or rewordings. The second type of change is probably the hardest; you may feel unwilling to give up a paragraph, or even a sentence. But revising is about keeping what works, and fixing or eliminating what doesn't. If it doesn't work, it detracts from the rest of your essay and needs to go.

Fulfilling the Assignment

On the largest scale, if your draft doesn't fulfill the requirements of the assignment, you need to figure out where you went wrong. Review your draft—where in your essay do you address the assignment and to what extent? Review your goal statement—does every component, including the evidence, the paragraph organization, etc., of your response fulfill the goal(s) you set out to accomplish? Highlight those sections of the essay that need additional attention, making sure to note why and how they are to be attended to.

Rewording Your Thesis

In Lesson 5, you learned about the three criteria of effective thesis statements—they must be argumentative, focused, and detailed. If your thesis isn't clear, or is not easily identifiable, you probably have one of these common problems:

- **No thesis.** Your essay may have a lot to say, but its paragraphs are not held together by one controlling idea. This type of essay is often the result of insufficient planning. If you took the time to consider your audience and purpose, brainstorm, and develop a tentative thesis and outline, you should be able to avoid this problem. Go back to your prewriting notes to find the main idea you started with, and begin drafting a thesis from there.
- **Your thesis isn't supported by your essay.** You do have a thesis, but the body of your essay supports another (perhaps similar) idea. This often happens when writers discover, through the drafting process, that they feel differently about their topic than they had originally thought. As a result, they end up building a case for a different thesis. If your essay supports an idea that's different from your thesis (and that idea still addresses the assignment), the easiest way to correct the problem is to rewrite your thesis to fit your essay.
- **More than one main idea.** If your essay has multiple main ideas, you may not have sufficiently narrowed your thesis during the planning stage. Recall in Lesson 5 the discussion concerning the need to have a thesis that correlates with the space confines of an essay. It must be broad enough to warrant an essay length discussion, and narrow enough to be able to complete a thorough discussion within those confines. Perhaps you discovered other interesting ideas while drafting and decided to include them; as a result, you have two or three underdeveloped mini-essays rather than one fully developed idea. If you have more than one main idea, see if there is a way to tie them together. Otherwise, choose the best one and revise your essay to develop that idea alone.

Thesis statements evolve and adapt as your essay evolves and adapts. Ask yourself, "Is my thesis aligned to the main ideas presented in the subsequent paragraphs?" If not, identify the gap and revise your thesis accordingly.

Checking for Support

You'll also need to assess how well your draft supports your thesis, and how well your evidence, examples, and details support the ideas you put forth. Types of support include:

- reasons
- facts
- specific examples
- descriptions and anecdotes
- expert opinions and analysis
- quotations from the text

How Much Is Enough?

There is no hard and fast rule about how much support you need for an effective essay, but remember this: *everything*, including your essay, is an argument—that is, an attempt to convince someone else of the merits of your beliefs. Have you offered enough support? Think in terms of persuasiveness, not amount.

Support That's Directly Related to the Thesis

Directly relevant thesis support is crucial. What good are ten supporting paragraphs if they're not supporting the right idea? Read the following essay carefully, paying particular attention to the support provided for the thesis.

When was the last time you told a lie? If you're like most people, it was probably recently. Did you know that you can also lie without even saying a word? This kind of lie can be even more devastating.

The poet Adrienne Rich said, "Lying is done with words and also with silence." To lie means "to tell something that is untrue." But it also means "to be deceptive." We often use silence to deceive. Rich is right. We lie with words, but also with silence.

Imagine a man who buys a necklace for his girlfriend from a thief. He knows the necklace is stolen and doesn't tell his girlfriend. She later finds out it's a stolen necklace when she tries to take the necklace back to the store for repairs.

I'm guilty, too. I knew my friend's boyfriend was seeing someone else. But I kept quiet. I helped keep her in the dark. Then, when she found him out—and found out that I'd known about it—it was terrible. It destroyed their relationship and our friendship.

Looking closely at the two supporting examples, you can see that neither one addresses how these silent lies are more devastating than a spoken lie. Now the writer must make a decision. Should she expand each paragraph to explain how keeping silent was worse than lying aloud? Or should she revise her thesis to eliminate the idea that silent lies are more devastating than regular lies?

Choosing the latter, she revised her thesis once more and created the following thesis statement:

We lie with words, but also with silence. And these lies can be equally devastating.

Now the writer has two solid supporting examples for her thesis. But she should probably add at least one, and preferably two more, to strengthen her essay.

Practice 1

Review an essay draft you composed from a previous lesson or for a current or recent assignment. Identify a body paragraph in the essay that lacks strong support or thesis connection, and revise your reasons and evidence to strengthen its relevance. Explain why you made the changes you did, and why they strengthen support for the thesis.

Strategies for Convincing

Before you consider your check for support complete, consider whether you've applied the strategies for convincing, as discussed in Lesson 10. Ask the following questions:

- Are your supporting paragraphs specific?
- Do you analyze the behaviors, beliefs, and values commonly associated with the topic?
- Do you acknowledge counterarguments?
- Do you make concessions and/or rebuttals?
- Do you qualify your claims?
- Do you assess the implications of the topic?

The examples in the *lying with silence* essay, for example, are not as specific as they could be. In fact, they would work better if they were expanded with more information that showed how people are affected by silent lies. Instead of one paragraph for each example, two or even three would bring the examples to life and make them more specific. Because the essay relies almost entirely on examples for support, the more detailed those examples are, the more convincing they will be.

Practice 2

On a separate sheet of paper or on your computer, revise one of the example paragraphs in the *lying with silence* essay to better address complexity by analyzing norms, qualifying claims, acknowledging counterarguments, or making connections. Expand the example until you have two complete paragraphs.

Summary

Revision deals with the content and style of your essay, and should begin by addressing the big picture issues—thesis and support. Look at your essay with fresh eyes, using trusted readers and rereading after taking a break from your writing. Then rework your essay to enure that it fulfills the assignment, contains a strong, clear thesis statement, and is supported with convincing examples and evidence.

Skill Building Practice

Use the read-aloud technique for an essay you're working on or that you wrote for another purpose. What did you notice about your writing? Do you like the way it sounds? Does it convey the meaning(s) you intended?

14 ▶ REVISING PARAGRAPHS

LESSON SUMMARY

This second lesson on the revision process shows you how to revise paragraphs for more effective organization and transitions. You'll also learn how to strengthen individual paragraphs.

The next step in revising examines your essay at the paragraph level. Ask a few big picture questions:

- Are your paragraphs in a logical and effective order?
- Does each paragraph have only one controlling idea?
- Are there effective transitions between ideas?
- Do special paragraphs fulfill their functions?

Checking Your Organization

If your ideas don't flow logically, they'll be difficult for readers to follow. Make sure your ideas are placed within your essay in an order that make sense. Follow the seven organizing principles discussed in Lessons 6 and 7:

- chronology
- order of importance
- spatial order
- classification
- cause and effect
- comparison and contrast
- problem → solution

As you read your paragraphs, checking carefully for organization, consider the following questions:

- **What organizing principle holds the essay together?** One overlying organizing principle should be clear. If you can't identify one, look carefully at how you presented your ideas. If you haven't used an organizing strategy, chances are your essay will feel disjointed to readers. Think about which strategy makes the most sense for your subject and purpose.
- **Is this the most effective organization for your subject and purpose?** Once you've identified your organizing principle, consider whether it's the best one for your essay. For example, if you've used the block technique for a comparison and contrast essay, you might consider whether the point-by-point method would work better instead.
- **Do any paragraphs or sections disrupt your organizational pattern?** If there is a break in your organizational structure, it should not only be intentional, but also serve a legitimate purpose. Perhaps you decided to keep the block comparison and contrast. However, in one section you slip into the point-by-point mode and compare two items directly. Unless there is a solid reason for this inconsistency, change that section to the block technique. Consistency makes your essay easier to read and understand.

Practice 1

Substantial revisions have been made to the *lying with silence* essay. For each paragraph, note the idea and function in the space provided. The first two paragraphs are done for you.

PARAGRAPH	IDEA	FUNCTION
When was the last time you told a lie? If you're like most people, it was probably recently. In fact, it was probably more recently than you think. The poet Adrienne Rich said, "Lying is done with words and also with silence." We don't have to talk to tell a lie. Our silences can be just as deceiving—and just as devastating.	Lying is also done with silence and can be devastating	Introduced the essay
You might be wondering how we can lie with silence. To lie means "to tell something that is untrue." But it also means "to be deceptive." There are many ways we deceive. Words are one way; silence is another.	Definition of lie	Explains how silence is also a lie
There's a difference between being silent because you don't want someone to know something and being silent because you want someone to think something that isn't true. The first is not a lie; it is not deceptive. The second, however, is a lie; the aim is to deceive. For example, imagine that I am in a job interview. If I don't tell you that I went to three different colleges, that's not a lie. But if I know you assume that I've graduated, and I don't tell you that I don't have a college degree, I am deliberately deceiving you with my silence. I am "telling" you a lie.		
These silent lies can have consequences. For example, a man who buys a stolen necklace for his girlfriend could lose her trust, which could be detrimental to the relationship. More importantly, he could also face criminal charges. In addition, even she could be in trouble for possession of a stolen necklace.		
This man has committed a crime with his silence. By remaining silent, he not only puts the woman in jeopardy for legal trouble, but he also can get in a lot of trouble himself.		
I'm guilty of silent deceptions, too. Last year, I discovered that my friend's boyfriend was seeing someone else. I kept quiet about it because I didn't want to hurt my friend. A few weeks later, someone else told her about the two-timing—and I told her I knew about it. She felt deceived, not only by her boyfriend, but by me, too. And those deceptions ruined her relationship with her boyfriend and our friendship.		

PARAGRAPH	IDEA	FUNCTION
Silent lies can also happen between strangers. Imagine you're at a diner. When the server hands you your check, you notice that she made a mistake, charging you $12.58 instead of $15.58. But you don't tell her. Instead, you pay the amount on the check, plus a tip based on that amount, and pocket the difference.		
These silent lies can cause as much harm as those told with words. They can even have devastating, serious consequences. That's why the law should not only prosecute people who lie on the stand, but also those who tell silent lies.		

Questions

Next, answer the following questions:

1. What is the main organizing principle of the essay?

   _____

2. Is this the best organizing strategy for the essay? Why or why not?

   _____

3. What would you suggest the writer do to improve the organization?

   _____

Revising Individual Paragraphs

To check the paragraphs that make up your essay, you'll need to examine your writing with a stronger lens than the one you used for "big picture" issues. You will be determining whether each paragraph has just one main idea, whether there are adequate transitions between paragraphs, and if your introductory and concluding paragraphs fulfill their distinct purposes.

One Controlling Idea

A paragraph is a group of sentences about one idea. That idea should be stated in a topic sentence, which is typically the first or last line. Topic sentences not only guide your reader, but they also link the sentences in the paragraph together by stating the idea that they all relate to. If you can't locate a topic sentence, should the main idea be stated in one, instead of implied by your examples?

If there is a topic sentence, does each sentence relate to it? In the *lying with silence* essay, each paragraph contains only one main idea, except for the sixth paragraph. Here, the writer describes the lie and its consequences in one paragraph. It would be more effective to dedicate another paragraph to the consequences. The revised paragraphing then looks like this (topic sentences are in bold):

I'm guilty of silent deceptions, too. *Last year, I discovered that my friend's boyfriend was seeing someone else. I kept quiet about it because I didn't want to hurt my friend. A few weeks, later, someone else told her about the two-timing—and I told her I knew about it.*

She couldn't believe that I deceived her like that. She felt just as betrayed as if I'd lied to her face about it. Her boyfriend's deception ruined their relationship. **My deception destroyed our friendship.**

Relevance

If you've identified more than one idea in a paragraph, you should probably break it into two paragraphs. But before you move text, make sure each idea is clearly related to the thesis. If it's not, it needs to be reworked or deleted. (If you didn't catch it when you were revising the big picture, here's another chance.) Remember the importance of maintaining focus in your essay—unrelated paragraphs not only get you off track, but also often confuse readers as well.

Development

Once you've identified the controlling idea of each paragraph, check to see that each idea is sufficiently developed. Topic sentences, like thesis statements, make assertions about your subject. And those assertions need support. Look carefully at any paragraph that consists of only one or two sentences. Chances are, they're seriously underdeveloped. The only time you should have a one-sentence paragraph is when you intentionally decide to emphasize the idea in that sentence.

Transitions

Transitions are the words and phrases used to move from one idea to the next. They help your words flow smoothly and show readers how your ideas relate to each other. In shorter essays, a phrase is usually enough to transition from one paragraph to the next. In longer essays, a sentence or two may be required to guide your reader to the next idea.

ORGANIZING PRINCIPLE	TRANSITIONAL WORDS AND PHRASES		
Order of importance	more importantly in addition first, second, third, etc.	above all first and foremost	moreover furthermore
chronological	then before while afterward first, second, third, etc.	next after as since	later during when until

spatial	beside	next to	along
	around	above	below
	beyond	behind	in front of
	under	near	
cause and effect	therefore	because	as a result
	so	since	thus
	consequently	accordingly	hence
comparison	likewise	similarly	like
	in the same way	just as	
contrast	on the other hand	however	on the contrary
	unlike	but	yet
	rather	instead	whereas
	although		

In the *lying with silence* essay, notice how the writer uses transitions to move from one paragraph to another. The first sentence of the sixth paragraph, "I'm guilty of silent deceptions, too" connects the previous example (the man who bought a stolen necklace for his girlfriend) to the next example, the writer's own silent lie. Then, the beginning of the second sentence uses the transitional phrase *for example* to lead readers into the support for that paragraph. In addition, the phrase *a few weeks later* provides a transition in the middle of the paragraph, connecting the writer's decision to keep silent with her friend's discovery of the deception.

To demonstrate how important transitions are, here's the fourth paragraph of the essay with transitions removed and then repeated with transitions intact (and underlined):

These silent lies can have consequences. A man who buys a stolen necklace for his girlfriend could lose her trust, which could be detrimental to the relationship. He could also face criminal charges. Even she could be in trouble for possession of a stolen necklace.

These silent lies can have consequences. <u>For example</u>, a man who buys a stolen necklace for his girlfriend could lose her trust, which could be detrimental to the relationship. <u>More importantly</u>, he could also face criminal charges. <u>In addition</u>, even she could be in trouble for possession of a stolen necklace.

Introductions and Conclusions

Both of these paragraphs must fulfill specific duties within the essay. While you're revising, you'll need to look closely at them to make certain they function properly.

As you reread your introduction, ask:

- Does it provide the context needed to understand my thesis?
- Does it clearly state the main point of my essay?
- Does it set the tone for the essay?
- Does it grab my reader's interest?

Notice how the introduction to *lying with silence* accomplishes each of these four tasks. It provides context by quoting Adrienne Rich's claim about silent deceptions. It clearly states the thesis in the last two sentences. It also sets the tone by using words like *deceives* and *devastating*, which will be repeated in the essay. In addition, it grabs the audience's attention by beginning with a thought-provoking question.

As you reread your conclusion, ask:

- Does it restate my thesis in a new way?
- Does it offer a new understanding?
- Does it provide a sense of closure?
- Does it arouse my reader's emotions?

While the *lying with silence* essay does a good job with the introduction, its conclusion needs work. Notice how it simply restates the thesis instead of putting it in different words. It does offer a new understanding, but goes too far by introducing a contentious new issue instead of providing a sense of closure.

Practice 2

On a separate sheet of paper or on your computer, revise the conclusion to the *lying with silence* essay.

In Short

To revise at the paragraph level, first check for your overall organizing principle. How have you arranged your paragraphs? Is this the most effective organizing strategy for your essay? Then check individual paragraphs to make sure they have only one relevant and fully developed idea. Next, check for transitions, both between and within paragraphs. Finally, check to see that your introduction and conclusion fulfill their important functions.

Skill Building Practice

Look again at the essay you read aloud at the end of Lesson 14. Identify the organizing principle, the topic sentences, and the transitions used throughout the essay.

15 ▶ EDITING

LESSON SUMMARY

Editing focuses on words and sentences. Are your word choices clear and direct? Are there any repetitive or awkward sentences or phrases? When you edit, you can revise words and sentences to make them better convey your intended meaning.

Unlike revising, which entails the possible reworking of large parts of your essay, editing is a word-by-word task. To edit your essay effectively, you'll need to read each paragraph a number of times, paying careful attention to your sentences and the words that comprise them. As you read your essay, ask yourself the following questions. Highlight any problems as you encounter them, along with any ideas about how to improve the problem(s):

- Are unnecessary words and phrases cluttering up your sentences?
- Do you repeat yourself?
- Are there any clichés, pretentious language, or confusing jargon?
- Do you use the active voice whenever possible?
- Do you avoid using ambiguous words and phrases?
- Are verb tenses consistent?
- Is the antecedent for every pronoun clear?
- Do you use precise adjectives and adverbs?
- Is your sentence structure varied?

Be Concise

Why use ten words to get across a meaning that could be better said in five? Those ten words will definitely waste your reader's time and probably confuse the point you're trying to make. Many of the words and phrases that follow are both well known and, unfortunately, well used. They don't convey meaning, and are therefore unnecessary. The following are three of the worst offenders, with usage examples.

1. *Because of the fact that*. In most cases, just *because* will do.
   - Because of the fact that he was late, he missed his flight.
   - Because he was late, he missed his flight.

2. *That* and *which* phrases. Eliminate them by turning the idea in a *that* or *which* phrase into an adjective.
   - These were directions that were well written.
   - These directions were well written.

3. *That* by itself is a word that often clutters sentences unnecessarily.
   - The newscaster said that there was a good chance that election turnout would be low and that it could result in a defeat for our candidate.
   - The newscaster said there was a good chance election turnout would be low and could result in a defeat for our candidate.

Word Choices for Concise Writing

WORDY	REPLACE WITH or DELETE
a lot of	many or much
all of a sudden	suddenly
along the lines of	like or such as
are able to	can
as a matter of fact	in fact or Delete
as a person	Delete
as a whole	Delete
as the case may be	Delete
at the present time	currently or now
both of these	both
by and large	Delete
by definition	Delete

Word Choices for Concise Writing (continued)

due to the fact that	because
for all intents and purposes	Delete
has a tendency to	often or Delete
has the ability to	can
in order to	to
in the event that	if
in the near future	soon
is able to	can
it is clear that	Delete
last but not least	finally
on a daily basis	daily
on account of the fact that	because
particular	Delete
somewhere in the neighborhood of	about or around
take action	act
the fact that	that or Delete
the majority of	most
the reason why	the reason or why
through the use of	through
with regard to	about or regarding
with the exception of	except for

Wordy and Concise Sentences

Wordy:	The students were given detention on account of the fact that they didn't show up for class.
Concise:	The students were given detention because they didn't show up for class.
Wordy:	Everyone who has the ability to donate time to a charity should do so.
Concise:	Everyone who can donate time to a charity should.
Wordy:	In a situation in which a replacement for the guidance counselor who is retiring is found, it is important that our student committee be notified.
Concise:	When a replacement for the retiring guidance counselor is found, our student committee must be notified.

Avoid Unnecessary Repetition

Unnecessary repetition is a sign of sloppy writing. It's easy to repeat the same thing, varying it slightly each time. It's harder to say something well once, and then write about your next idea or example. Repetition also wastes valuable time and space. If you are writing while the clock is ticking, or are limited to a number of words or pages, say it right the first time and move on.

For example:

Repetitive:	They met at 4 P.M. in the afternoon.
Concise:	They met at 4 P.M.

P.M. means in the afternoon, so there's no reason to say *in the afternoon*. It's a waste of words and the reader's time.

Repetition can be found even in short phrases. The list that follows contains dozens of such phrases that can clutter your essay. Most of them contain a specific word and its more general category. Why state both? The word *memories* can only refer to the past, so you don't need to say *past memories*. We know that blue is a color, so describing something as *blue in color* is repetitive and therefore unnecessary. In most cases, you can correct the redundant phrase by dropping the category and retaining the specific word.

Some of the phrases use a modifier that is unneeded, because the specific is implied in the general. For instance, the word *consensus* means general agreement. Therefore, modifying it with the word *general* is repetitive. Similarly, *mathematics* is a field of study, so it does not need to be modified with the word *field*. You can tighten up your writing, saying it well one time, by eliminating wordiness.

RETAIN ONLY THE FIRST WORD		DROP THE MODIFIER (FIRST WORD)	
any and all	**odd** in appearance	~~past~~ memories	~~terrible~~ tragedy
first and foremost	**mathematics** field	~~final~~ destination	~~end~~ result
refer back	**cheap** quality	~~general~~ consensus	~~final~~ outcome
close proximity	**honest** in character	~~various~~ differences	~~free~~ gift
large in size	**confused** state	~~each~~ individual	~~past~~ history
often times	**modern** in design	~~basic~~ fundamentals	~~totally~~ obvious
reason why	**unusual** in nature	true facts	~~rarely~~ ever
heavy in weight	**extreme** in degree	~~important~~ essentials	~~unexpected~~ surprise
period in time	**strange** type	~~future~~ plans	~~sudden~~ crisis
round in shape	**blue** in color		

Avoid Overly Informal and Overused Language

People communicate in so many ways and in so many mediums these days that it's not altogether unexpected to see language better suited for a text message end up in a formal essay. When you're assigned an essay, think about the connection between the assignment's purpose and your language; your purpose is likely to analyze, reflect, or convince. Also be sure to think about your audience. Use the appropriate language in your essay, and avoid words and phrases that are too colloquial, obscure, or confusing.

Slang

Slang is nonstandard English. Its significance is typically far removed from either a word's denotative or connotative meaning, and is particular to certain groups—therefore, it will likely exclude some readers from understanding it. It is also inappropriate and offensive to use slang terms for racial or religious groups.

Clichés

Clichés should be avoided, not only because they are too informal, but also because they are overused. Your writing should be in your own voice, without relying on stale phrases such as *one step at a time, no news is good news, have a nice day,* and *no guts, no glory.*

Vulgar Language

The last thing you want to do is turn off or offend your reader. Since it's difficult to know what kind of language your audience may find offensive or in poor taste, err on the side of caution by not including any language considered even mildly obscene, gross, or otherwise offensive.

Think Twice Before Opening Your Thesaurus

Big words won't win points with your readers. Aim to sound like yourself, not to impress with your knowledge of ten-letter words. Here are three reasons to stop looking for and using so-called big words.

1. They sound pretentious (you're supposed to sound like you, not a politician or chairman of the board).
2. They can sound ridiculous (by using words that are not in your normal vocabulary, you run the risk of using them incorrectly).
3. They may appear as a tactic (your reader might think you are trying to add weight with words because you are worried your essay isn't well written or that your ideas aren't worth reading).

To the point: *I decided to keep it simple by packing only those things that I could carry in one suitcase.*
Thesaurized: *I determined to eschew obfuscation by packing only those things that I could transport in one valise.*

To the point: *At my summer job, I had the chance to learn about Information Technology as it relates to engineering.*
Thesaurized: *At my summer employment, I had the fortuity to obtain IT-related information as it pertains to the engineering field.*

Use the Active Voice

Verbs have two voices. In the **active voice**, the subject is the source of, or cause of, the action. In the **passive voice**, the subject is acted upon. In a personal essay, you are usually the subject. That means the active voice is much more effective in conveying your personality through your essay—you're the "actor," not the "acted upon." The active voice is also clearer and more direct. In the following examples, note the simplicity and directness of the first sentence in each pair. The second sentences, written in the passive voice, are clunky and noticeably longer.

Compare:
My friend asked for another helping.
Another helping was asked for by my friend.

I misplaced my wallet.
My wallet was misplaced by me.

The administration has selected three finalists for the open position.
Three finalists for the open position have been selected by the administration.

Avoid Ambiguity

Ambiguous means having two or more possible meanings. Ambiguous language can either be words and phrases that have more than one meaning, or word order that conveys a meaning different from the one intended by the writer:

The quarterback liked to tackle his problems.

This sentence can be read two ways: The quarterback likes to *deal with* his problems, or his problems are his opponents on the field whom he *grabs and knocks down*. This kind of confusion can happen whenever a word has more than one possible meaning. *The quarterback liked to address his problems* is a better sentence, and is unlikely to be misunderstood.

My advisor proofread my essay with the red sports car.

Here, the *word order* of the sentence, not an individual word, causes the confusion. Did the advisor proofread the essay with his car? Because the phrase *with the red sports car* is in the wrong place, the meaning of the sentence is unclear. Try instead: *My advisor with the red sports car proofread my essay.*

Clear Up Confusing Pronoun References

Pronouns (words such as *I, we, them,* and *her*) take the place of nouns. They should only be used when the noun to which they refer (known as the **antecedent**) is obvious and meaningful. Check the pronouns in your writing to be certain they are not one of the following:

- unclear
- too far from the antecedent
- useless

Correcting Ambiguous Language

Ambiguous: *When doing the laundry, the phone rang.*
Clear: The phone rang when I was doing the laundry.

Ambiguous: *She almost waited an hour for her friend.*
Clear: She waited almost an hour for her friend.

Ambiguous: *I told her I'd give her a ring tomorrow.*
Clear: I told her I'd call her tomorrow.

Ambiguous: *A speeding motorist hit a student who was jogging through the park in her blue sedan.*
Clear: A speeding motorist in a blue sedan hit a student who was jogging through the park.

More Examples of Pronoun Usage

Incorrect: Both Fellini and Bergman edited *his* movie.
Correct: Both Fellini and Bergman edited *Bergman's* movie.

Incorrect: Leave all ingredients out of the recipes *that do not belong* in a healthy diet.
Correct: Leave all ingredients *that do not belong* in a healthy diet out of the recipes.

Incorrect: They banned parking in their lot so the snowplows could do their job.
Correct: *The owners of the parking lot* banned parking in their lot so the snowplows could do their job.

Incorrect: The Civil War and the Spanish-American War took place in the nineteenth century. *It* was a turning point for the country.
Correct: The Civil War and the Spanish-American War took place in the nineteenth century. *The Civil War* was a turning point for the country.

Example: *Trini is interested in teaching and farming, which is her career choice.*

What is her career choice? *Which* could mean either teaching or farming, making it unclear. The writer needs to restate the career instead of using a pronoun in order to eliminate the possibility the reader will not understand the sentence. *Trini is interested in teaching and farming, but farming is her career choice.*

Example: *They always talk about the dangers of global warming.*

This common pronoun error is known as an **expletive**: *They* is useless, because it appears to refer to no one. If the writer has that information, he or she can revise the sentence to be more precise: *The newspaper frequently has articles about the dangers of global warming.* If there is truly no *they,* the sentence should be revised by eliminating it: *There is much talk about the dangers of global warming.*

Practice 1

Edit the following paragraph for clarity. Eliminate wordiness, unnecessary repetition, overly informal or over-used language, the passive voice, and ambiguity.

I believe that the biggest and greatest challenge my generation will face will be ethical dilemmas created by scientific discoveries and advances. There has been a boatload of things discovered in this century, especially in the time period of the last few decades. Humankind is able to avail itself of a plethora of opportunities it heretofore was unable to take advantage of. But some very difficult ethical questions have been raised by these opportunities. They have given us new power over nature, but this power can easily be abused and misused.

Use Modifiers to Add Precision

Modifiers make your point clear while adding meaning and originality to your writing. Consider how powerful, specific adjectives and adverbs work in these sentences:

Sentence A: My grandmother put on her sweater.
Sentence B: My grandmother put on her *cashmere* sweater.

Sentence A: The football team practiced in the rain.
Sentence B: The football team practiced in the *torrential downpour*.

In both cases, sentence B allows you to better hear the voice and impressions of the writer, giving a more accurate and interesting picture of the action.

The right modifiers (adjectives and adverbs) can also get your message across in fewer words. This is critical in an essay with a specified length. You don't want to sacrifice unique details, but sometimes, one word will do the job better than a few. For example, *Chihuahua* can take the place of *little dog*; *exhausted* can take the place of *really tired*; and *late* can take the place of *somewhat behind schedule*.

Vary Your Sentence Structure

The repetition of sentence patterns is not only boring, but in some cases, it can reduce your grade. The SAT essay, for example, is scored by readers trained to look for, and reward, variety in sentence structure. They can deduct a point or two for an essay filled with sentences that follow the same pattern. When you're editing your essay, check for monotonous sentence structure. Here's an example:

The plasma membrane is the outermost part of the cell. It isolates the cytoplasm. It regulates what comes in and out of the cytoplasm. It also allows interaction with other cells. The cytoplasm is the second layer of the cell. It contains water, salt, enzymes, and proteins. It also contains organelles like mitochondria.

Notice how each sentence begins with a noun or pronoun, followed by a verb. The rhythm created by this repetition is boring. A successful edit should vary the sentences:

The plasma membrane, the outermost part of the cell, isolates the cytoplasm. It regulates what comes in and out of the cell and allows interaction with other cells. The second layer, the cytoplasm, contains water, salt, enzymes, and proteins, as well as organelles like mitochondria.

The edited version combines sentences and uses introductory phrases and **appositives** (descriptive words and phrases set off by commas) to vary sentence structure. The result is a much more engaging paragraph.

Practice 2

Edit the following paragraph, replacing general words with more exact ones and creating variety in sentence structure. (Note: You may also have to revise for clarity to address some of the problems in this paragraph.)

My generation will have many problems. One is the feeling of being overwhelmed by technology. Another is that the generation gap is growing. Another is that there are more people than ever before. There isn't enough room for everybody. There are also limited resources.

In Short

Wordiness and ambiguity often prevent ideas from coming across clearly. Edit your sentences to eliminate clutter and unnecessary repetition. Revise sentences that use overly informal or overused words, and exchange the passive voice for the active. Clarify ambiguous words and unclear pronoun references. Finally, improve your writing by using precise modifiers and adding variety to your sentence structure.

Skill Building Practice

Try writing some bad sentences. Use unnecessary words and repetition, jargon, pretentious words, unclear pronoun references, and ambiguous words. Avoid exact words and phrases, and repeat the same sentence structure. By trying to write poorly, you'll get a better sense of what to avoid in your writing.

16 ▶ PROOFREADING

LESSON SUMMARY

Before you submit your essay, there's one more important step—*proofreading*. Good proofreading involves far more than a simple running of spell and grammar check on your computer. This lesson explains how to use these tools to your advantage, as well as how to find and correct the most common errors in grammar and mechanics.

Studies on grammar- and spell-check programs show that they are more effective when used as a first (not final) step in proofreading. After you've clicked your mouse through grammar and spell check, print out a hard copy of your essay and complete your proofreading. Check for errors in grammar and mechanics.

Limitations of Spell and Grammar Checkers

There is no excuse for not using spell- and grammar-check programs. They're fast and simple, and catch many common errors. However, they're not foolproof. Spell check has three important limitations you should be aware of:

1. **Non-Word versus Real-Word Errors**

   Most of us think of spelling errors in the first category—that is, a string of letters that does not make a real word. You might type *sevn* instead of *seven*, or *th* for *the*. Spell check is an excellent tool for catching these types of mistakes. However, if you are discussing the seven years of piano lessons you have taken, and you leave off the *s* in the word *seven*, the result is *even*, which spell check won't flag, because *even* is correctly spelled.

This is known as a real-word error. You have typed a legitimate, correctly spelled word; it's just not the word you meant to type, and it doesn't convey the meaning you intended. Spell check can't find these types of errors.

2. Proper Nouns

Spell check uses a dictionary that does not include most proper nouns and words in other categories, such as the names of chemicals. You can always add a word or words to the dictionary once you are sure of its spelling, but the first time, you will need to use another source to verify the spelling.

3. Errors Spelled Similarly to Other Real Words

If you misspell a word in such a way that it is now closer, letter by letter, to a word other than the one you intended, spell check will probably offer the wrong word as a correction. For example, if your essay includes a coffeehouse scenario, and you type the word *expresso*, spell check will correct the error with *express* rather than *espresso*. Similarly, *alot* will be corrected to *allot*. You must pay careful attention to spell check's suggested corrections to ensure the right selection.

Grammar-check programs are also effective but not foolproof. They can make two kinds of mistakes: missing errors, and flagging errors that are actually correct. The first problem, missing errors, is illustrated by the following examples. A grammar check on the following sentence did pick up the subject/verb agreement error (*I is*), but did not notice the participle error (*I studying*).

I is ready to take the exam after I studying my notes and the textbook.

Similarly, the punctuation problems in the following sentence were not flagged.

The recipe, calls for fifteen ingredients and, takes too long to prepare.

When grammar check does highlight an error, be aware that it may in fact be correct. But if your knowledge of grammar is limited, you will not know whether to accept grammar check's corrections. To further complicate matters, you may be offered more than one possible correction, and will be asked to choose between them. Unless you are familiar enough with the specific problem, this may be no more than a guess. It is important to understand the type of error highlighted, and get more information if you are not sure about it.

Professional Proofreading Tricks

1. **Take your time.** Studies show that waiting at least 20 minutes before proofreading your work can increase your likelihood of finding errors. Get up from your computer, take a break, or move on to some other task, and then come back to your writing.

2. **Read backward.** Go through your writing from the last word to the first, focusing on each individual word, rather than on the context.

3. **Ask for help.** A pair of fresh eyes may find mistakes that you have overlooked dozens of times, and one or more of your colleagues or friends may be better at finding spelling and grammar errors than you are.

4. **Go under cover.** Print out a draft copy of your writing, and read it with a blank piece of paper over it, revealing just one sentence at a time. This technique will encourage a careful line-by-line edit.

5. **Watch the speed limit.** No matter which proofreading technique(s) you use, slow down. Reading at your normal speed will not give you enough time to spot errors.

6. **Know thyself.** Keep track of the kinds of errors you typically make. Common spelling errors can be caught by spell check if you add the word or words to the spell-check dictionary. When you know what you are looking for, you are more likely to find it.

Proofreading for Grammar

Grammar refers to the hundreds of rules that govern sentences. Space confines limit this book's discussion of those rules to three of the most common errors:

- confusing words (*they're, there, their*)
- agreement (singular nouns with singular verbs, plural nouns with plural verbs)
- run-ons and sentence fragments

Confusing Words

Often, words are confused because the writer is in a hurry. It's not a matter of needing to learn the meaning of the words, but rather taking the time to check for accuracy. However, certain groups of words are commonly confused because not only do they sound or look alike, but also their meanings may be close enough to cause hesitation. Check the following list for those you're unsure of, and commit that shorter list to memory.

WORD	DEFINITION OR USAGE
accept (*verb*) except (*prep.*)	to recognize excluding
affect (*verb*)	to influence
effect (*noun*)	result
effect (*verb*)	to bring about
among (*prep.*) between (*prep.*)	to compare three or more people or things used for two people or things
beside (*adj.*)	next to
besides (*adv.*)	in addition to
complement (*noun*)	match
compliment (*noun, verb*)	praise; to give praise
desert (*noun*) dessert (*noun*)	arid, sandy region sweet served after a meal
e.g.	abbrev. for Latin *exempli gratia* (*free example* or *for example*)
i.e.	abbrev. for Latin *id est* (*it is* or *that is*)
elicit (*verb*) illicit (*adj.*)	to stir up illegal
farther (*adv.*)	beyond
further (*adj.*)	additional
imply (*verb*) infer (*verb*)	to hint or suggest to assume, deduce
its (*pronoun*)	belonging to it
it's (*contraction*)	contraction of *it is*
Hint: Unlike most possessives, it doesn't have an apostrophe.	
lay (*verb*)	the action of placing or putting an item somewhere; a transitive verb, meaning something you do *to* something else
lie (*verb*)	to recline or be placed (a lack of action); an intransitive verb, meaning it does not act on anything or anyone else

WORD	DEFINITION OR USAGE
loose (*adj.*)	not restrained, not fastened
lose (*verb*)	to fail to win; be deprived of
principal (*adj.*)	main
principal (*noun*)	person in charge
principle (*noun*)	standard
stationary (*adj.*)	not moving
stationery (*noun*)	writing paper
than (*conj., prep.*)	in contrast to
then (*adv.*)	next
that (*pronoun*)	introduces a restrictive (or essential) clause
which (*pronoun*)	introduces a nonrestrictive (or nonessential) clause

Hint: Imagine a parenthetical *by the way* following the word *which*. "The book, which (by the way) Joanne prefers, is her first novel," is incorrect. Therefore, it should read, "The book that Joanne prefers is her first novel." "Lou's pants, which (by the way) are black, are made of leather," is correct.

their (*pronoun*)	belonging to them
there (*adv.*)	in a place
they're (*pronoun*)	contraction for *they are*
who (*pronoun*)	substitute for *he, she,* or *they*
whom (*pronoun*)	substitute for *him, her,* or *them*
your (*pronoun*)	belonging to you
you're (*pronoun*)	contraction for *you are*

Agreement

Agreement refers to the balance of sentence elements such as subjects and verbs, and pronouns and antecedents. (An **antecedent** is the noun a pronoun replaces.) To agree, singular subjects require singular verbs, and plural subjects require plural verbs. Likewise, singular nouns can be replaced only by singular pronouns, and plural nouns require plural pronouns.

Most of these errors are easy to spot. If you mistype "The scientists was working on an important experiment," you (or, possibly, your grammar-check program) will catch it. But problems arise when a phrase or phrases separate the subject and verb or noun and pronoun. Here's an example:

"Eat, drink, and be merry," is a label associated with Greek philosopher Epicurus, but like most catchy slogans, they simplify what is actually a rich and complex message.

Notice how the phrase *like most catchy slogans* can mislead you. If you assume *slogans* is the subject, then the pronoun *they* and the verb *simplify* seem correct—they agree with the plural subject. But look again at the sentence. *Slogans* isn't the subject of the verb *simplify*. What is simplifying? Not the *slogans*, but the *label "Eat, Drink, and Be Merry"*—a singular noun. Thus, the pronoun must be *it* and the verb must be *simplifies* to agree with the subject.

Run-ons and Sentence Fragments

Complete sentences require a noun and verb, and express a fully developed thought. Two common sentence errors are extremes. **Sentence fragments** stop too quickly; they are phrases that are not whole thoughts. **Run-on sentences** don't stop soon enough; they include two or more complete clauses or sentences.

Sentence fragments are often missing a subject or verb, and may be phrases or parts of other sentences. Be aware that fragments can sometimes be difficult to identify because even though they don't express complete thoughts, they can be long and appear correct. Here are a few examples, with corrections:

Incorrect:
Because she had to stop studying and go to lacrosse practice.
Cried a lot.
When we finished the game after the sun began setting.

Correct:
She had to stop studying and go to lacrosse practice.
Sheu Ling cried a lot.
We finished the game after the sun began setting.

Run-on sentences are made up of two or more independent clauses or complete sentences placed together into one sentence, without proper punctuation. For example:

We were hungry and John was tired so we had to stop at the first rest area that we saw.
Kim studied hard for the test that's why she got an A.
Patty took flying lessons every Saturday so she couldn't go to the picnic and she couldn't go to the graduation party either but she has already signed up for another group of flying lessons because she likes it so much.

Here's how to fix run-on sentences:

1. Separate the clauses with a **period**. Example: *We are here. You are not.*
2. Connect the clauses with a **comma** *and* a **conjunction** (*and, or, nor, for, but, so, yet*). *We are here, but you are not.*
3. Connect the clauses with a **semicolon** (and possibly an adverb such as *however, therefore*, or *otherwise*, making sure it expresses the right relationship between the two ideas). *We are here; you are not.*

The previous run-ons can be corrected as follows:

We were hungry and John was tired, so we had to stop at the first rest area that we saw.
Kim studied hard for the test; that's why she got an A.
Patty took flying lessons every Saturday, so she couldn't go to the picnic. She couldn't go to the graduation party either, but she has already signed up for another group of flying lessons because she likes it so much.

Practice 1

Proofread the following paragraph for grammatical mistakes. Make changes to improve the clarity and structure of the sentences as well.

Comic relief is important in tragedies, readers need a little relief from all of the sadness in the story. For example, Hamlet. Ophelia had just died. The next seen is with the gravedigger. Who is a very funny character. They dug up a skull and makes along speech about who the skull might have belonged to. Even though its about death. The scene is funny, it lets readers forget about the tragedy for a moment and laugh.

Proofreading for Mechanics

Mechanics refers to the standard practices for the presentation of words and sentences, including capitalization, punctuation, and spelling. As with grammar, there are many rules for mechanics, but here we will cover the ones that cause essay writers the most problems. See the Appendix for more thorough grammar and mechanics resources.

Capitalization

Capitalization is necessary both for specific words and to start sentences and quotes. However, many writers overuse it. Only six occasions require capitalization:

1. the first word of a sentence
2. proper nouns (names of people, places, and things)
3. the first word of a complete quotation, but not a partial quotation
4. the first, last, and any other important words of a title
5. languages
6. the pronoun *I*, and any contractions made with it

Punctuation

There are dozens of punctuation marks in the English language. They're used to separate ideas, form words, and make the meanings of sentence clear. Poor punctuation can confuse your readers and change your intended meaning. For example, one comma completely changes the meaning of this short sentence:

Don't call me, stupid!

Don't call me stupid!

Here's a quick punctuation review:

IF YOUR PURPOSE IS TO:	USE THIS PUNCTUATION:	EXAMPLE:
end a sentence	**period [.]**	Use a period to end a sentence.
connect complete sentences	**semicolon [;]** or a **comma [,]** and a **conjuction** [*and, or, nor, for, so, but, yet*]	A semicolon can connect two sentences; it is an excellent way to show that two ideas are related.
connect items in a list	**comma [,]** but if one or more items in that list already has a comma, use a **semicolon [;]**	The table was overturned, the mattress was torn apart, and the dresser drawers were strewn all over the floor. The castaways included a professor, who was the group's leader; an actress; and a housewife.
introduce a quotation or explanation	**colon [:]** or **comma [,]**	Colons have three functions: introducing long lists, introducing quotations, and introducing explanations. He said, "This simply won't do."
indicate a quotation	**quotation marks [" "]**	"To be or not be?" is one of the most famous lines from *Hamlet*.
indicate a question	**quotation mark [?]**	Why are so many engineering students obsessed with *Star Trek*?
connect two words that work together	**hyphen [-]**	brother-in-law, well-known author
separate a word or phrase for emphasis	**dash [—]**	I never lie—never.
separate a word or phrase that is relevant but not essential information	**parenthesis [( )]**	There is an exception to every rule (including this one).
show possession or contraction	**apostrophe [']**	That's Jane's car.

Spelling

Proofreading for spelling errors after you've run a spell-check program means looking carefully for real-word errors. If you typed *tow* instead of *two*, that mistake is still in your essay, waiting for you to find it. Use the professional proofreading tricks on page 133 (especially numbers 2, 4, and 6) to scan for mistakes.

Practice 2

Proofread the following paragraph for mechanical errors:

Compact discs (CDs), which may be found in over 25 million american homes not to mention backpacks and automobiles first entered popular culture in the 1980's. But there history goes back to the 1960's, when an Inventor named James Russell decided to create and alternative to his scratched and warped phonograph records, a system that could record, store, and replay music without ever whereing out.

In Short

Proofreading is the final step in the writing process. Begin by running spell- and grammar-check programs, being mindful of their shortcomings. Then, using the professional proofreaders' tips, study your essay for errors in grammar. In particular, look out for confused words, agreement mistakes, and run-on sentences and fragments. Finally, check your mechanics. Have you used capital letters and punctuation marks correctly? Are there real-word or other spelling errors that spell check missed?

Skill Building Practice

Review a recent essay draft you completed and identify any grammar and/or mechanics concerns that surface repeatedly; explain what grammar or mechanics rules you had difficulty following, and correct the errors you made.

4 ▶ TAKING AN ESSAY EXAM

T his fourth and final section deals with a specific essay-writing situation: the timed essay exam. You can use most of the writing strategies you've learned so far, but because your time is limited, this kind of essay requires a unique approach. The lessons in this section will give you specific strategies for tackling essay exams, from the crucial planning stage through the editing process.

17 ▶ PREPARING FOR AN ESSAY EXAM

LESSON SUMMARY

Essay exams are stressful. You have to come up with a well-written piece under a strict time restraint in a room crowded with other students. How can you alleviate some of that stress and walk into the testing room with confidence? The answer is preparation.

Writing an essay in an exam situation, with the clock ticking, is very different from other types of essay writing. Of course, the fundamentals of good writing don't change (which is why Sections 1–3 apply to any type of essay). What changes is your approach. When you have just 25 minutes (SAT), 30 minutes (ACT), or an hour (many state tests, such as Regents'), you must use your time wisely. Every minute counts.

The way to take full advantage of every minute is to prepare; gather all available information about the test beforehand, checking the resources in the Additional Resources section of this book, as well as your exam's website. Understand the type of prompt you'll find on the test, know how to organize your thoughts, and be able to expand prewriting notes into paragraphs. Take timed practice exams not only to get used to the situation, but also to identify your strengths and weaknesses. When you take a timed essay exam, preparation can mean the difference between a great score and a poor one.

PREPARING FOR AN ESSAY EXAM

Types of Exams

Spend time learning the general features of the essay you'll be taking. Understand the topics and what scorers will be looking for. Study the instructions for your essay carefully (they're all online)—think of how much time you'll save during the exam if you don't have to read them. Finally, visit the test website to get the most up-to-date information about topics and any changes made to the tests.

ACT

The ACT Plus Writing Test is optional. Some schools require the test, so check with those you plan on applying to before you make your decision to register for it. The essay is written in response to a prompt concerning an issue of relevance to high school students. You'll need to take a stand on that topic, support your point of view, and present a counterargument.

Here's a sample prompt:

In an effort to reduce juvenile violence and crime, many towns have chosen to enforce curfews on minors under the age of eighteen. These curfews make it illegal for any minor to loiter, wander, stroll, or play in public streets, highways, roads, alleys, parks, playgrounds, or other public places between the hours of 10:00 P.M. and 5:00 A.M. These curfews also make it illegal for parents or legal guardians to allow minors to congregate in certain public places unsupervised. Those who support these curfews believe they would reduce community problems such as violence, graffiti, and drugs, and would force parents and guardians to take responsibility for their children's whereabouts. Those who oppose curfews for minors claim these laws violate the Fourteenth Amendment rights of life and privilege for U.S. citizens. They also believe that such curfews stereotype minors by presupposing that citizens under the age of eighteen are the only people who commit crimes.

In your essay, take a position on this paragraph. You may write about either one of the two points of view given, or you may present a different point of view on this topic. Use specific reasons and examples to support your position.

Two trained readers will score your essay on a scale of 1–6; the highest possible score is a 12, and the lowest is a 2. Those readers will evaluate how well you:

- supported your position
- maintained focus on the topic
- developed and organized your position logically
- supported your ideas
- adhered to the rules of standard written English

For the latest information about the test, check www.act.org.

GED

The General Educational Development (GED) test contains a 45-minute writing section, in which test takers must develop an expository essay that includes personal observations, knowledge, and experience. The typical GED essay is about 250 words in length, written on your choice of five topics. A list of possible topics, as well as some test-taking hints, may be found at www.cdlponline.org. The official GED Testing Service website offers links to your jurisdiction's testing program, which may differ slightly from that of other states. Check www.acenet.edu for the latest information.

Those who score the GED essay read between 25 and 40 essays an hour. They look for:

- well-focused main points
- clear organization
- development of ideas
- appropriate sentence structure and word choice
- correct punctuation, grammar, and spelling

SAT

With just 25 minutes to write, you won't be expected to turn in a final draft essay when taking the SAT. Minor errors in grammar, usage, and mechanics are not weighed against you. Scorers instead read the essay to get an overall impression of your writing ability. They look for evidence of critical thinking: how well you responded to the topic, developed a point of view, and used appropriate examples and evidence to support your position. Is your essay clearly focused, and does it transition smoothly from one point to the next? Do you show evidence of having a varied and intelligent vocabulary?

You'll get either a "response to a quote" or a "complete the statement" prompt. The former has one or two quotes on a topic—you'll need to take a stand on that topic in your essay. The latter asks you to fill in the blank in a sentence, and write an essay based on your completed sentence. The latest information on the SAT essay may be found at www.collegeboard.com.

Regents' and Other Exit Exams

More than 25 states, including California, Alaska, North Carolina, and Texas, require a passing grade on an exit exam to be eligible for high school graduation. These tests vary, so it is important to get specific information about the test you are preparing to take. However, most exit exams allow 60 minutes to develop an essay based on one of a choice of topics. A list of topics for Georgia's Regents' exam, for example, may be found at www.gsu.edu (but remember to check with your school regarding the test you will be given).

A typical exit essay is approximately 1,500 words. Possible topics include responses to literature, biographical narratives, and even business letters. Those who grade exit essay exams ask:

- How well did you address the topic?
- Were your ideas organized?
- Did you develop major points, and support them with details and examples?
- Were your word choices and sentence structure effective and varied?
- How consistent was your style (paragraphing), grammar, spelling, and punctuation?
- Did you express yourself freshly and uniquely?

Types of Essays

You have been assigned dozens of essays during high school. They might have been a response to something you read, an argument about a particular topic, or an explanation of an event or other subject of study. In fact, there are countless types of essays. However, almost all timed essay exams fall into one of two major categories: expository or persuasive. In fact, the ACT and SAT call exclusively for persuasive essays.

Expository

An **expository** essay gives directions, instructions, or explanations. It informs by presenting the writer's knowledge about the topic to the reader. You might be asked to *define*, *compare* and/or *contrast*, or *explain* cause and effect. In fact, think of the verbs used in your topic as *key words* that clue you in to the fact that you are being asked to write an expository essay. These key words include:

- **Compare:** examine qualities or characteristics to note and discuss similarities and differences
- **Contrast:** examine two or more ideas, people, or things, stressing their differences
- **Define:** give a clear, authoritative meaning that identifies distinguishing characteristics
- **Describe:** relate the details that make the subject in question unique
- **Diagram:** create a graphic organizer that explains your answer
- **Discuss:** examine the subject(s) thoroughly, and give a detailed explanation of its strengths and weaknesses
- **Enumerate:** determine the points you must make, and present them in a list or outline form
- **Explain:** clarify meaning in a straightforward fashion, paying attention to the reasons for a situation
- **Illustrate:** use examples, graphic organizers, evidence, or analogies to give meaning or answer a problem
- **Interpret:** explain the meaning of something or solve a problem using personal opinions, judgments, or reactions
- **List:** see *enumerate*
- **Narrate:** explain an occurrence by describing it as a series of chronological events
- **Outline:** describe in an organized fashion, systematically, highlighting only the major points (details not necessary)
- **Relate:** explain the associations or connections between two or more things, events, circumstances, or even people; may also be used to mean *narrate* (see *narrate*)
- **Recount:** see *narrate*
- **Review:** critically examine the topic, event, idea, or thing in question, discussing major points and their strengths and/or weaknesses
- **State:** express major points concisely, without using examples or details
- **Summarize:** see *state*
- **Trace:** similar to *narrate*; describe the chronology of an event to reveal its meaning

The Best Way to Achieve a High Essay Score

The scorers of every type of timed essay agree on one significant point: You must support your essay with details, examples, and evidence. Not only will they strengthen your argument, but they will make your writing come alive. Common advice for essay exam takers is to include at least one sentence in each paragraph that begins with the words. Compare the following:

High school seniors should be allowed open campuses, on which they can arrive in time for their first class, leave during free periods, and come back to school for their other classes. There is no reason to treat high school seniors like children by making them stay in school all day when they don't have classes to attend all day. Seniors can handle the extra responsibility.

High school seniors should be allowed open campuses, on which they can arrive in time for their first class, leave during free periods, and come back to school for their other classes. Seniors are given freedom and responsibility in many other areas of their lives; for example, the ability to drive a car. Seniors are also permitted to vote, and to prepare for their futures through the college admissions process or vocational training.

The first example uses generalizations and unsubstantiated claims ("no reason to treat [them] . . . ," "can handle the extra responsibility"), which weaken the argument. The second uses evidence, such as the responsibility of driving and voting, to make the case for open campuses. Remember to back up what you say with evidence, details, and other types of examples.

Persuasive

In a **persuasive** essay, you choose one idea and show why it is more legitimate or worthy than another. Your purpose is not to merely show your side, but to convince your reader why your side is best. In order to convince effectively, you must base your argument on reasoning and logic. The most important strategy for the persuasive essay is to choose the side that has the best, or most, evidence. If you believe in that side, your argument will most likely be even stronger (although you don't have to believe in it to write a good essay).

An important component of a persuasive essay is the inclusion of other sides or points of view. In fact, the scoring rubric for the ACT essay notes specifically that readers will be looking for counterarguments. Counterarguments are presented in order to be refuted or weakened, thereby strengthening the case for your side. However, it is important to use reasoning and understanding to refute them. If you don't sound fair, or simply present emotional reasons why your side is best, you have weakened your argument. You must show that your idea is most legitimate in part because other ideas are weak or incorrect.

Key verbs that will help you identify a call to write a persuasive essay include:

- **Criticize:** express your judgment about the strengths and weaknesses of your topic, and draw conclusions
- **Evaluate:** assess the topic based on its strengths and weaknesses, drawing conclusions
- **Justify:** defend or uphold your position on the topic, using convincing evidence
- **Prove:** confirm or verify that something is real or true using evidence, examples, and sound reasoning

Understanding Your Prompt

This advice might seem obvious, but it aims to correct one of the most common mistakes made on essay exams. Spend time understanding the type of prompt you'll encounter. Remember that your score depends in large part on how well you address that prompt (both the ACT and SAT essay directions note that an essay written off topic will be scored 0; a GED essay that fails to adequately address the prompt also gets the lowest score—a 1). Preparation materials, both in print and on the Internet, are available for every essay exam, so it's easy to familiarize yourself with them.

Many students fail to address the prompt because they didn't understand what it was asking them to write about. The best way to determine whether you understand it is to put the prompt in your own words, and then compare yours with the original. Are they nearly the same in meaning? If you have trouble with this exercise, try circling the verbs (key words) in the original prompt. These are the same key words you will look for during the exam. When you understand the key words, you can more easily write the type of essay required by the prompt.

Budgeting Your Time

As you prepare to take your exam, familiarize yourself with its timing. Whether you have 25 minutes or an hour, you should complete three distinct tasks: planning, writing, and revising. The writing stage will take the longest, and, for essays that don't hold grammatical and spelling mistakes against you, the revising stage will be the shortest. But every essay should include all three.

Planning

Section 1 covered prewriting. Review in particular Lessons 3 and 4, and decide, based on a few practice essays, which brainstorming technique works best for you in a timed situation. Knowing exactly what you will do when you begin the exam will not only help you save time, but will also take some of the pressure off, too. Some exit exams (such as Indiana's Graduation Qualifying Exam) judge your prewriting notes, outlines, and other graphic organizers, making it even more important to choose a strategy that you know you do well ahead of time. Even if you are taking the SAT, and have just 25 minutes for your essay, spend the first 4–7 minutes planning.

Your planning time, no matter which prewriting strategy you use, should involve the formation of a thesis statement and three or four main points. Any supporting evidence for, or examples of, those points should be included. Once you begin planning, don't be tempted to switch topics, which will waste valuable writing time. Allow a few minutes to think through the topic. You may cross off main points that don't work, or add a new one or two as you go.

Time Management

Set a schedule that allows for each step in the writing process. The following is a typical plan for essay time management:

- Spend the first ¼ of your time planning your essay.
- Spend ½ of your time drafting your essay.
- Spend the last ¼ of your time editing and proofreading your essay.

Practice

Set a timer for seven minutes. Using any of the brainstorming methods from Lesson 3 or 4, draft a thesis statement for the following sample SAT essay prompt:

Some people say there are no more heroes, but I see plenty of heroic people all around me. One person I consider a hero is _____.

Fill in the blank in the sentence. Write an essay in which you explain your answer.

In Short

The time you spend planning for and preparing to take an essay exam can mean the difference between a great score and a poor one. Do your homework by researching your exam: Understand how it's scored, what type of prompt(s) you'll encounter, what the directions say, and even how much space you'll be given to write in. Learn how to respond quickly to a prompt by practicing. Brainstorm ideas and develop a thesis statement and outline in just five minutes or less.

Skill Building Practice

Gather a couple of sample prompts online or from other books about your exam (see the Additional Resources section for a list of books and online resources). Set the timer for five minutes and practice brainstorming ideas and writing thesis statements and outlines. The more you practice, the easier it will be to plan your essay on exam day.

18 ▶ DRAFTING, EDITING, AND PROOFREADING

LESSON SUMMARY

This lesson explains how to spend your time drafting, editing, and proofreading your essay.

You've prepared for your essay and understand what it should look like (including the instructions), and how it will be scored. You've practiced brainstorming ideas and drafting thesis statements from sample prompts. Now, it's time to write and refine your essay.

Drafting

Because you're writing under a strict time restraint, essay scorers don't expect your essay to be perfect. However, they don't expect a sloppy first draft that needs plenty of revising, either. Think instead of creating a "polished rough draft;" writing that's more refined than a typical rough draft, well organized, and with as few errors in grammar and mechanics as possible.

General Guidelines

- Use your brainstorming as a guide. Don't go off on tangents, but adhere to your plan. If you come up with another strong major point, use it, but don't freewrite or ramble.
- Separate your major points into paragraphs; this organization will help your readers follow the logic of your argument.
- Avoid unnecessary words, phrases, and sentences. Don't repeat yourself or try to fill space with meaningless phrases such as "this is a very interesting question" or "different people have different opinions on this subject."

Editing and Proofreading

The revision step is not included in this lesson for an important reason. Revising takes too much time and involves too much shuffling of text to be accomplished in the time you're given to write your essay. Recall instead that essay exams should be "polished rough drafts." There won't be extra minutes to move sentences from one paragraph to another, delete chunks of information, or add many new points (and even if you did have the time, you'd create a mess that most readers wouldn't be able to make sense of). That's why it's critical to spend time brainstorming ideas and to adhere to them once you begin drafting. An extra sentence or two inserted later to clarify a point is fine, but there isn't the space or time to allow for a real revision. Instead, focus on editing and proofreading your essay.

Timed exams only penalize for grammar, spelling, punctuation, and other errors in mechanics when it impairs understanding. All exams take off points for incomplete answers and failure to address the prompt. Leave some time to go over your work and correct or improve any errors. Be prepared to spend between 2–5 minutes editing and proofreading your essay. Check for the following:

In Paragraphs

1. details, examples, and supporting evidence in each paragraph
2. incomplete thoughts that could negatively affect your essay
3. rambling, off-topic thoughts
4. paragraph breaks that help the reader see your main points
5. effective transitions between ideas

In Words and Sentences

1. complete sentences (no fragments or run-ons)
2. variety in sentence structure
3. agreement
4. concise word choices
5. clichéd, pretentious language
6. ambiguity

7. passive voice
8. proper punctuation and capitalization
9. correct spelling

Practice

Set aside 20 minutes for this exercise. Resist the urge to read ahead and think about the exercise before you're ready to complete it. When you're ready, set a timer and take the essay exam on the next page.

Hints for Taking any Essay Exam

- Get a good night's sleep and eat a good meal before the exam.
- Bring all required items (such as writing instruments, identification, and/or a receipt).
- If there is a choice, read the prompts quickly to find the one you can think of the most examples and evidence for.
- Don't change your mind after making your prompt selection.
- Underline the key words in your prompt.
- Write legibly. You won't get points for neatness, but if they can't read it, they can't score it.
- Wear a watch, and make a plan for budgeting your time.

"Ignorance is bliss." Write an essay in which you agree or disagree with this statement. Use an example from your personal experience, current events, history, literature, or another discipline to support your point of view. Use the following space to write your answer. You may use a scrap piece of paper to formulate ideas and take notes. Do not write on any other topic; do not skip lines.

In Short

On an essay exam, you need to write a "polished rough draft." Follow your outline and write carefully but quickly. Make sure your thoughts are complete and your handwriting is neat. Don't repeat yourself, or use filler words and phrases. Choose words that concisely and clearly convey your ideas. Leave a few minutes to edit and proofread your essay, correcting any mistakes you might have made.

Skill Building Practice

Like all skills, your ability to write well under pressure will improve with practice. Chose one of the essay topics from the introduction of this book, set a timer for 30 minutes, and write another essay!

19 ▶ SAMPLE ESSAY EXAM QUESTIONS AND ANSWERS

LESSON SUMMARY

This final lesson presents two sample essay exam assignments and several sample responses. The responses are analyzed to give you a clearer sense of what constitutes a high- and a low-scoring essay.

When you're faced with any new task, it's helpful to see how others have successfully completed it. That's why this final lesson is devoted to sample essay prompts and responses. There are two sample exams, based on the kinds of prompts used on the ACT, GED, Regents', and SAT exams. Five answers are given that cover a range of scores.

It's important to understand *why* each response received the score it did. You can study the scoring rubric for your exam either online or in a book, but you'll learn more by seeing what essays at each level look like. Our rubric (which may be found in the answer key) is based on those used to score the ACT, GED, Regents', and SAT essays.

Sample Essay Exam #1

The photograph or picture that moved me the most is _____.

Assignment: Visual images have the power to inspire thought, evoke emotion, create mood, and even make political statements. Complete the statement and write an essay that explains your choice of image. You may choose any image, including a family photograph, famous work of art, drawing or painting done by a friend, or even a book illustration. Support your choice by using appropriate examples and details.
Time allowed: 25 minutes

Sample Response #1

You might think a memorable picture would have vivid color, an appealing or inspirational theme, or be something you might want to display and look at every day. That is not the case with the picture that is most memorable to me. Rather, it is a large mural, painted in 1937 by the Spanish artist, Pablo Picasso, to protest the bombing of a small village in northern Spain.

Surprisingly, there is no vivid red color to show the flowing blood. One must imagine this, for the mural is startlingly gray, black, and white. But there is no avoiding the horror of the images. The figures are not realistically drawn, but are cubist and abstract, and it is apparent that innocent civilians are being slaughtered. A mother screams with her mouth wide open, her head tipped back in heart-rending anguish, as she holds her dead baby. A soldier lies dead on the ground, clutching his broken sword, and three other people are shown in shock and agony. Animals, including a tortured horse and a crying bird, are also portrayed as innocent victims of the massacre.

Some symbols are open to interpretation. What is the meaning of the bull, which seems simply to be observing, or of the light bulb emitting rays at the top of the mural? Does the bull symbolize brute force, and does the light bulb signify that there is hope? Yet there is no doubt that the distorted, horrible images are intended to shock the viewer. This depiction of human grief is a profound statement of the cruelty and senselessness of war. Limiting the picture to black and white adds a funereal element to the shocking depiction of the catastrophe.

The memory of the picture cannot be forgotten; it is a metaphor for the senselessness and the horror of war. While it was painted to protest atrocities in a long ago war, it is as relevant today as the recollection of the horrors of September 11. Perhaps it should be shown to all those who contemplate starting a war. Would it be worth it to have another Guernica?

Assessment

On a scale of 1–5, this essay received a score of 4. While the writing skills are effective, the organization could be improved. For example, the fact that the painting is black and white is mentioned in the second and third paragraphs, both times noting how the color choice adds to the mood of the painting. Paragraph 3 has a number of major points; it would be less confusing if each point had its own paragraph.

There is a clear point of view, and the writer has obviously studied not only the painting, but the language of art criticism as well. Examples are well chosen and numerous. Word choice is varied and sophisticated, and there are very few errors in grammar and mechanics. If the essay were better organized, and the writer had followed the five-paragraph form, it could have received a score of 5.

Sample Response #2

The picture I remember is Guernica. It is by Picasso. It is not reelist. That means the shapes don't look real but you know what they are in real life. It is in black and white. It is not in color like most pictures. But it really gets to you. It shows people getting killed or who are already killed. The images make it so you won't forget it.

What this picture does is to make you know that war kills people and it is just awful. A baby is killed and a soldier is killed. A mother is screaming because her baby is dead. It kills people and it kills animals and even if you are not killed you will probly be screaming or crying. There are lots of ways that life gets destroyed by war. The painting shows many of them.

This picture could be for any war it doesn't matter. In that way it is a universal message. There is not anything in the picture that tells you where it is happening. You don't know who the people are. There are wars hapening today. People suffer now like in Guernica. You remeber it because it makes you upset and you wish there would never be a war. Then people wouldn't have to suffer. This picture is memrable because you remember how the people suffered and they probly didn't do anything.

Assessment

On a scale of 1–5, this essay received a 2. Organizationally, it has three paragraphs and each contains a main idea. However, two of them also include the introduction and conclusion. While they don't detract from or confuse the author's ideas, there are numerous errors in grammar and spelling. Most sentences are very short, and the lack of variety detracts from the essay. A strong point of view is maintained, but it gets lost in the unsophisticated and overly informal vocabulary.

Sample Essay Exam #2

An influential person is one who leaves a footprint in the sand of our soul. To me, the most influential person I can think of is _____.

Assignment: Complete the sentence above with an appropriate phrase. Then write an essay supporting your completed statement.
Time allowed: 45 minutes

Sample Response #1

Have you ever imagined how your life would be different if a key person were not in it, like a mother, father, spouse, or child? Some people are so integral to making us who we are that without them, our very identity would be changed. My grandmother is a key figure in my life who has left an indelible impression on me. She is a woman of great influence because of her stability, her work ethic, and her independent spirit.

Grandma is the matriarch of our family. Because she has a close relationship with us and a great deal of wisdom, her seven children and 16 grandchildren often seek her out for advice. We look to her for advice on everything from how to potty-train a toddler to how to break up with a boyfriend. Grandma relishes the fact that we ask her for advice, but she never offers it without being sought out. She is like a rock: never changing. My own parents got divorced when I was 12, but I always knew that Grandma's house was a source of stability when the rest of my world seemed tumultuous. This sense of security has helped me face other challenges as they come along in life, like when we moved during my freshman year of high school.

Grandma also inspired me to pursue my goals. Because of the trials she faced without shrinking back, I am able to have the strength to work hard and try to realize my dreams. Grandma didn't have it easy. Because she was a single parent from a fairly young age, she had to work and sacrifice to support her children. She worked full time cleaning offices to save for her children's college educations. She received no help from the outside and was totally independent from her own family's help. Grandma always stressed the importance of education to all of us in achieving our goals. Grandma's example of hard work and her emphasis on education have strengthened me to pursue a college degree, and eventually a PhD. Even though I will have to work to get through school, I know that if Grandma worked while raising seven children alone, I can handle taking care of myself. Her tireless example is truly inspirational. She has also encouraged me in my chosen career, teaching, because she feels it will blend well with family life when I eventually have my own children.

Perhaps the most significant legacy Grandma has left me is her example of always voicing her opinion despite what others may think. Grandma would never bow down to prejudice; she never cared what people would say behind her back. In an age where segregation in social circles was common, Grandma's dinners after church on Sundays would look like a United Nations meeting. She would include all races and nationalities, and became close friends with a very diverse group of people. If someone tried to put down another race, she would quickly voice her disagreement. This refusal to be swayed by "popular" opinion had a huge impact on me, and is a guiding principle in my life today.

I certainly would not be the person I am today, inside or out, without the influence of my grandmother upon my life. I can only aspire to imitate her in her stability, her work ethic, and her refusal to be silenced by other people's disapproval.

Assessment

On a scale of 1–5, this essay received a 5. It shows an insightful understanding of the assignment. The writer chose a strong example of an influential person, and then skillfully developed her ideas with specific examples. We learn much about Grandma, and the writer constantly connects these details back to the main idea: that Grandma had a huge impact on her life in three major areas. The writer shows an excellent command of language. There are no grammatical errors, and she varies her sentence structure to make the reading interesting and enjoyable. This essay fully addresses all areas of the rubric in a strong way and is a good example of clear competence in writing.

Sample Response #2

When someone comes into our lives for a long time, he or she leaves a footprint on our soul. I would say the biggest footprint in my soul comes from my little brother, Mario. Even though we've never had a conversation, Mario is a very big influence for three main reasons.

Mario is a peaceful person. He has a brain disease called lissencephaly. That happens when the brain is not bumpy and grooved like it's supposed to be. He has been like this from birth, and there's no cure. But Mario is like a little angel. He sits in his wheelchair and plays with his toys. Even though he is 8 years old, he can't walk or talk. But he has an inner peace that shines in his eyes. He never seems to worry about anything. He hardly ever cries or gets upset. He isn't impatient like the rest of us. He just takes each day, each hour, each minute as it comes. He has taught me about being peaceful no matter what is going on around me.

Mario has also taught me about unconditional love. Unconditional love means you love someone not because of what they can do for you, or what they have done for you, but just because you love them.

Mario also has influenced me to enjoy the simple gifts in life. I can run, walk, talk, and learn. Most of my friends complain about homework, girlfriends, and petty, stupid fights with their friends. But Mario, without saying anything, reminds me that it's all good. I have more than he does, and I should be content with what I have. I don't need to have the newest CD or my own car to be happy.

Not many people have a special gift like Mario in their life. I am really lucky because he has influenced me, I think, to be a better person. I've learned a lot about life from him, how to live and how not to live.

Assessment

On a scale of 1–5, this essay received a 3. The student shows a basic understanding of the assignment, using the example of his brother Mario to develop a response to the prompt. There is good development, particularly in the second paragraph, with specific examples. However, the second body paragraph, about unconditional love, is unsupported. Detracting from the essay are a very basic vocabulary and little sentence variety. This is a fair response with good ideas that would benefit from more sophisticated grammar and vocabulary, and more concrete support.

Sample Response #3

My mother is the person who influenced me the most. She is a very hard worker. She is a very devoted mother, and she is tough.

My mother works at Macy's, cleaning the rest rooms and straightening up the stock after the store closes. It is not an easy job, she does it from 12 midnight til 8 in the morning. My mother wanted to go to college, but her parents didn't have no money. She really want us to all go. I would love to make her proud of myself. That would be a great reward to her for all she did for us.

My mother cares about all the things that no other mothers pay no attention to anymore. She won't let me hang out with my friends without calling, no boys in the house when she's not home, I have to cook and clean, etc. She is a very devoted mother.

One day, some lady almost ran me over in front of my house. My mother went out there and tryd to find what the cause was. Well, the lady starting screaming at my mother, and she was the one at fault! My mother yelled back and even called the cops on this lady, she isn't afraid of anybody.

I think I will probably turn out to be just like my mother, and that would be fine with me.

Assessment

On a scale of 1–5, this essay received a 2. It shows a basic understanding of the assignment, but little development. The writer lays out three ways her mother has been influential in her life, but then fails to adequately develop them with examples. In the second body paragraph, the writer never makes a connection between her mother's strictness and being a devoted mother. In addition, she doesn't really discuss how this has affected her. There is a weak introduction with no real "hook," and a short conclusion that weakens the organization of the essay. The sentences are simple and contain noticeable errors, particularly run-on sentences. Overall, this response shows marginal competence in writing.

Practice

Assess the essay you wrote for the practice exercise in Lesson 19. On a scale of 1–5, how would you rate your essay? What are its strengths? What are its weaknesses? Identify the things you did well in your essay. Then, list the ways you think your essay could be improved.

Congratulations!

You've completed 19 lessons and have learned much about how to write essays that are more effective. To see just how much your skills have improved, turn the page and take the posttest. You should see a dramatic difference in your understanding of the writing process and in your ability to write clearly and effectively in an essay format.

To keep your skills sharp, write regularly. Start a journal or blog, write letters to friends, take a composition class, or join a writer's group. In addition, pay attention to what you read. Your writing will be positively influenced by good writing. See the Additional Resources section for more suggestions.

POSTTEST ▶

To gauge how much your essay-writing skills and your understanding of the writing process have improved, take the following posttest. Though the questions differ from those on the pretest, the format and material covered are the same, so you will be able to directly compare results.

When you complete the test, check your answers, and then compare your score with the one you received on the pretest. Your new score should be significantly higher, but if it's not, review the lessons that teach the skills on which you tested poorly. Whatever your score, keep this book on hand for reference as you continue on your academic journey.

You can use the space on the pages following Part 2 to record your answers and write your essay. Or, if you prefer, simply circle the answers directly for Part 1.

Take as much time as you need for Part 1 (although 20 minutes is an average completion time). When you're finished, check your answers against the answer key at the end of this book. Each answer tells you which lesson deals with the concept addressed in that question. Set aside another 30 minutes to complete Part 2.

1. (a) (b)
2. (a) (b) (c) (d)
3. (a) (b) (c) (d)
4. (a) (b) (c) (d)
5. (a) (b) (c) (d)
6. (a) (b)
7. (a) (b) (c) (d)

8. (a) (b) (c) (d)
9. (a) (b) (c) (d)
10. (a) (b) (c) (d)
11. (a) (b) (c) (d)
12. (a) (b) (c) (d)
13. (a) (b) (c) (d)
14. (a) (b) (c) (d)

15. (a) (b)
16. (a) (b) (c) (d)
17. (a) (b) (c) (d) (e)
18. (a) (b) (c) (d)
19. (a) (b) (c) (d)
20. (a) (b) (c) (d)

Part 1

1. If your essay is well written, there's no need to completely fulfill the assignment.
   a. true
   b. false

2. In general, you should write for which audience?
   a. your classmates
   b. your teacher, admissions officer, or exam reader
   c. yourself
   d. a general reader

3. Which of the following introductory tasks does this introduction fail to do?
   In this essay, I would like to consider why the Great Depression occurred. Some people contend that it was caused by the stock market crash of 1929. Many economists point to the Smoot Hawley Tariff Act as the real reason. However, there is strong evidence to suggest that neither of these factors caused the Great Depression.
   a. provide context
   b. state the thesis
   c. grab the reader's attention
   d. set the tone for the essay

4. In the following paragraph, which is the topic sentence?
   Too much sun can produce many negative consequences. First, it can dry your skin, which in turn reduces its elasticity and speeds the aging process. Second, too much sun can burn unprotected skin and cause permanent discoloration and damage to the dermis. Most importantly, long-term exposure of unprotected skin can result in skin cancer.
   a. the first sentence
   b. the second sentence
   c. the third sentence
   d. the fourth sentence

5. Which two organizational strategies does the paragraph in question 4 use?
   a. order of importance and comparison/contrast
   b. cause/effect and chronology
   c. classification and chronology
   d. order of importance and cause/effect

6. Three supporting ideas should be sufficient for any essay assignment.
   a. true
   b. false

7. A single-sentence paragraph is appropriate if
 a. you don't have any support for the assertion in that sentence.
 b. you have too many long paragraphs throughout the essay.
 c. it's a particularly well-written sentence.
 d. you want to emphasize the idea in that sentence.

8. Read the following essay assignment carefully. Which of the sentences best describes the kind of essay that you should write?
In Civilization and Its Discontents, *Freud explains why he believes civilized people are unhappy. Summarize his theory and evaluate it.*
 a. Describe the main points of Freud's theory and assess the validity of that theory.
 b. Define "civilization" and show examples of civilized communities.
 c. Describe several examples that illustrate Freud's theory.
 d. Describe the main points of Freud's theory and express your opinion about his theory.

9. When revising an essay, which of the following issues should you address first?
 a. grammar and spelling
 b. organization and transitions
 c. thesis and support
 d. introductory paragraph

10. Which of the following sentences has the most effective word choice?
 a. She was scared.
 b. She was petrified.
 c. She was frightened.
 d. She was scared stiff.

11. Which of the following would be a problem in a concluding paragraph?
 a. It doesn't restate the thesis.
 b. It frames the essay.
 c. It arouses the reader's emotions.
 d. It doesn't bring up any ideas that aren't related to the thesis.

12. Which of the following is typically the best organizational strategy in an argument?
 a. order of importance (least to most important)
 b. order of importance (most to least important)
 c. cause and effect
 d. comparison and contrast

13. Identify the grammatical problem in the following sentence.

After he mastered the trumpet, he learned the guitar, and then learned how to play the piano, he went on to become one of the greatest jazz pianists in the world.

   a. sentence fragment
   b. agreement
   c. run-on sentence
   d. incorrect word choice

14. On an essay exam, most of your time should be spent
   a. planning.
   b. drafting.
   c. proofreading.
   d. editing.

15. An introduction should never be more than one paragraph long.
   a. true
   b. false

16. What is the main problem with the following sentence?

After his fight with Alan, he swore he would never let anyone use his car again without his permission.

   a. It's a run-on sentence.
   b. It's not properly punctuated.
   c. It's unnecessarily wordy.
   d. Its pronouns may be confusing.

17. A thesis should be which of the following?
   a. short
   b. clear
   c. assertive
   d. both **a** and **b**
   e. both **b** and **c**

18. Outlining should typically occur
   a. before you brainstorm.
   b. after you brainstorm.
   c. after you write your first rough draft.
   d. before you revise.

19. Which of the underlined words in the following paragraph are transitions?
Too much (1) *sun can produce many negative consequences.* <u>First</u> (2), *it can dry your skin, which in turn reduces its elasticity* <u>and</u> (3) *speeds the aging process.* <u>Second</u> (4), *too much sun can burn unprotected skin and cause permanent discoloration and damage* <u>to the dermis</u> (5). <u>Most importantly</u> (6), *long-term exposure of unprotected skin* <u>can result in</u> (7) *skin cancer.*
  a. 1, 2, and 3
  b. 2, 4, and 5
  c. 2, 6, and 7
  d. 2, 4, and 6

20. Credibility is best established by which of the following?
  a. expertise and freedom from bias
  b. expertise and education
  c. education and bias
  d. reputation and freedom from bias

Part 2

Set a timer for 30 minutes. When you're ready to begin, read the essay assignment that follows carefully. Use the space provided to write your essay. Stop writing when 20 minutes have elapsed, even if you haven't completed your essay. When you're finished, look at the scoring chart in the answer key to estimate your essay's score.

Essay Assignment
Many people feel that a movie isn't a success if it doesn't force viewers to think about an important issue or idea. Others argue that movies are successful as long as they entertain us; they don't have to have any ideological, political, or social agenda. What do you think? Is being entertaining enough? Or should movies do more? Why? Provide specific examples to support your position.

_____

_____

_____

_____

_____

_____

_____

_____

_____

ANSWER KEY ▶

This section provides answers, sample answers, and explanations for the pretest, practice exercises, and posttest. Use the answers and explanations to assess your understanding of the lessons. But keep in mind that many of the exercises call for a written response, and those responses will be different for each person who completes the exercises. Suggested answers will demonstrate how one student successfully completed the assignment.

Pretest, Part 1

If you miss any of the answers, you can find help for that question type in the lesson(s) shown to the right of the answer.

QUESTION	ANSWER	LESSON
1.	b.	11
2.	c.	8, 12
3.	d.	12
4.	a.	1
5.	a.	16
6.	d.	6, 7
7.	b.	2
8.	c.	6
9.	b.	5, 8

QUESTION	ANSWER	LESSON
10.	b.	9
11.	c.	10
12.	a.	13
13.	d.	15
14.	c.	18
15.	a.	3, 4
16.	b.	14–17
17.	e.	10
18.	b.	9, 15
19.	c.	16
20.	d.	11

Pretest, Part 2

Use the following scoring chart to evaluate your essay. First, score your essay yourself (don't worry if some of the requirements are unfamiliar—a highly accurate score is not as important as the practice you received in writing a timed essay). Then, ask someone else (an English teacher or a friend with strong writing skills is ideal) to score it. After you assign a number for each of the categories shown on the chart, average the numbers to get an overall score.

CHARACTERISTIC	5	4	3	2	1
Response to Assignment	Completely fulfills the assignment; may go beyond the requirements to a new level.	Fulfills all of the requirements of the assignment.	Fulfills most of the requirements of the assignment.	Fails to fulfill a major part of the assignment.	Does not fulfill the assignment.
Thesis	Is clear, asserative, and original.	Is clear and assertive.	Is suggested but may be weak or unclear.	Is weak and/or unclear.	No recognizable thesis.
Development	Several strong supporting ideas are offered; each idea is thoroughly developed.	Several supporting ideas are offered; most are adequately developed, but one or two are underdeveloped.	Offers some supporting ideas but not enough to make a strong case; ideas may be underdeveloped.	Few supporting ideas are offered; the ideas that are provided are insufficiently developed.	Little or no support is offered; ideas are poorly developed.

CHARACTERISTIC	5	4	3	2	1
Focus	All ideas are directly and clearly related to the thesis.	Most ideas are directly and clearly related to the thesis.	A majority of ideas are related, but there are some loose connections and/or digressions.	Some focus, but many ideas are unrelated.	No focus; most ideas are unrelated to the thesis or topic.
Argumentation	Addresses counterarguments, makes concessions, and establishes credibility.	Adresses most counterarguments, establishes credibility for most sources; may neglect to make concessions.	Adresses some counterarguments but may neglect some major counterpoints; establishes credibility for some sources.	Fails to address most counterarguments; does not establish credibility for most sources; does not make concessions.	Does not address counterarguments, establish credibility, or make concessions.
Organization	Ideas are well organized; structure is clear; provides strong transitions throughout.	Ideas are well organized; good transitions throughout most of esssay.	Essay has organizing principle, but pattern may be disrupted; some ideas are out of order; some transitions may be weak or missing.	Organizing principle may be unclear; many transitions are missing.	No organizing principle; weak or missing transitions throughout the essay.
Sentences	Ideas come across clearly; variety in sentence structure.	Most ideas are clear; may occasionally be wordy.	Sentences may be cluttered with unnecessary words or repetition; ambiguity may interfere with clarity.	Sentences are often wordy or ambiguous, interfering with clarity.	A majority of sentences are wordy or ambiguous, often interfering with clarity.
Word Choice	Precise and careful word choice; avoids jargon and pretentious language.	Most words are exact and appropriate; an occasionally ineffective word choice.	Mix of general and specific words; some pretentious language or jargon.	Mostly general inexact words; word choice sometimes inappropriate.	Word choice often ineffective or inappropriate.
Grammar	Virtually error free.	A few grammatical errors, but none that interfere with clarity.	Several grammatical errors; may interfere with clarity.	Many grammatical errors; often interfere with clarity.	Most sentences have grammatical errors, often interfering with clarity.
Mechanics	Virtually error free.	A few mechanical errors, but none that interfere with clarity.	Several mechanical errors; some may interfere with clarity.	Many mechanical errors that interfere with clarity.	Most sentences have mechanical errors that interfere with clarity.

Lesson 1

Practice 1

SUBJECT	DIRECTIONS
change in citizen's attitudes toward federal government in last decade	describe
what I think caused this change	explain
impact of this attitude on power of government	assess

Practice 2

SUBJECT	DIRECTIONS
whether Celie has control over her destiny	answer and explain

Practice 3

Answers must include a verb that specifies the goal. For example:

My goal is to explain the conflict that Hughes felt and show how he resolved his conflict.

Lesson 2

Practice 1

A successful response might look like this:

Assignment:	Discuss how sports influence popular culture. Use specific examples from the sports world.
Broad topic:	How sports influence popular culture
Narrowed topic:	How sports influence trends in fashion
Sufficiently narrowed topic:	How sports influence fashion and how sports heroes contribute to the rise of a highly profitable sneaker industry

Practice 2
Responses will vary. Here is a possibility:

Assignment:	Identify a factor that you believe figures strongly in a childs' personality
Broad topic:	Factors influencing a child's personality development
Narrowed topic:	Parents
Sufficiently narrowed topic:	Parents who work outside the home
Further narrowed topic:	What kind of childcare working parents choose affects a child's personality development.
Topic turned into a question:	How does the kind of childcare that working parents choose affect their child's personality development?
Tentative thesis:	

Lesson 3

Practice 1
Answers will vary. Here's one possibility:

When I was in the ninth grade, it was chemistry class, the first exam, and a lot of people were cheating. They all had cheat sheets and were even passing them back and forth. I was new, and I made some friends but wasn't really close to anyone, and I studied hard for the exam. I was really angry. The teacher looked up once or twice but didn't see anything. I was having trouble with one of the problems and thought about cheating, too. But I didn't have a cheat sheet. I knew if I told on the cheaters, it would mean trouble—didn't want to be an outcast. After the test, I typed a note and put it on the teacher's desk. Ms. Waller confronted us the next day—tensions were high! Cheaters were looking around trying to figure out who told—being new was lucky because no one suspected me—they blamed Pearl. Got really mean. I felt guilty. I confessed to Rob. But he ended up telling. Next day was one of the worst in my life. Someone threw food at me in the cafeteria, and everyone started calling me "rat," and worse. That name has stuck with me for two years, and it hasn't been easy making friends. I don't know if I'd do the same thing again. It's so hard to know what is the right thing to do, and how to fit in at the same time.

Practice 2

Here's an example:

A strong determining factor for my sense of identity is being a Vietnamese American.

- a strong determining factor for my sense of identity is being a Vietnamese American.
- one language for home and neighborhood, another for school
- can't always express myself with American friends
- my parents get mad when I forget how to say something in Vietnamese
- having to serve as translator for my parents
- my accent
- how hard it was to learn to read English
- shyness, esp. in classroom
- people assuming I don't speak English
- stereotypes—I don't always eat rice!
- feeling most comfortable with other Vietnamese Americans

Lesson 4

Practice 1

Here is one example:

SAMPLE CUBING FOR "SCHOOL UNIFORMS" PROMPT

Describe:	Requiring students to wear school uniforms used to only be an issue in religious schools; however, I know that many schools in cities are requiring a bland dress code to discourage gang violence or to make sure students don't dress too provocatively.
Compare:	I suppose it could be seen as an issue of free speech and the right to express one's self, but I think a more appropriate comparison are school security issues like metal detectors, pat-downs, and/or locker searches—all are about the challenges of creating a safe environment.
Associate:	I suspect those who oppose a mandated dress code imagine a soulless school where students are zapped of energy, as if robots; on the other hand, I imagine supporters see order, calm, and well-behaved children. It's hard not to imagine teenagers on one side of this issue and parents on another.
Analyze:	Seems like an issue with basic characteristics—students wear the same colored shirt and dress pants every day; it seems like it's not the act but the intent behind where the issue lies. The cause is misperception of one group in the community about another group's intent or purpose. I'm not sure you can really say that uniforms can directly impact things like violence or grades.

SAMPLE CUBING FOR "SCHOOL UNIFORMS" PROMPT

Apply:	If uniforms were to be mandated in my school, I can see a lot of complaining by students, perhaps some acts of rebellion here and there, but would it change how students interact in the halls or how they do in their studies? I doubt it. Our teachers and friends and hallways would be the same.
Argue:	Because they do not significantly alter or improve students' ability to learn, mandating uniforms is not an effective means of improving schools.

Lesson 5

Practice 1

1. **The death penalty is a controversial issue.**

   This statement is not argumentative; it is also not descriptive. One possible way of constructing a thesis that is argumentative and stays true to the author's original intent to analyze the issue rather than pick a side is to state, "Neither the pro-capital punishment nor the anti-death penalty camps have offered a satisfyingly persuasive argument on moral and political grounds."

2. **What would be the consequences of censorship on the Internet?**

   This is a question, not a position statement. An easy way to correct this is to simply answer the following question: "Censorship of the Internet would lead to great reductions in the kinds of rule-breaking, user-generated content, stifling not only artistic creativity but political expression as well."

Practice 2

An example response might state:

1. A film review serves to provide readers with an overview of the film's plot, its relationships, and a discussion of its merits as art and/or entertainment. Readers want to glean some sense of what the movie is about, whether its content or ideas connects with their interests, and whether the film is worth seeing.

2. I will be reviewing *Transformers* and focusing on plot and dialogue, two constant problems of big Hollywood blockbusters. My goal will be to explore how movies such as *Transformers*, in spite of their complex back stories and multiple characters, are glib and cringe-inducing.

SAMPLE CUBING FOR "MOVIE REVIEW" PROMPT

Describe:	Every summer, moviegoers are deluged with big, loud blockbusters sure to be full of great visual effects and lousy plots, scripts, and acting. *Transformers* is no exception; its computer-enhanced effects are fabulous, but every other component is contrived and cheesy.
Compare:	The previous movies in the *Transformers* series set the standard, but it sure seems like every movie these days fits the same profile—absurd premise, rowdy band of misfits, silly humor, a lot of explosions, and no character development. The endless string of sequels each summer is testament to this cliché.
Associate:	I know these films are made for and marketed to children, but they wouldn't be making so much money if it weren't for adults and film geeks—and that makes me wonder if these films are intentionally bad. The fact that these films always have a frantic editing and an over-stimulated visual style always makes me think of video games before cinema.
Analyze:	The fundamental problem with films like *Transformers* is two-fold. First, they always have plots that, in spite of the illusion of mythos, are basically the same dumb "good-versus-evil-quest-over-some-mystical-object" plot we've seen for decades. Second, their continued reliance on superficial archetypes ensures a significant and cold distance between audience and character.

SAMPLE CUBING FOR "MOVIE REVIEW" PROMPT

Apply:	Movies that are both escapist and insightful have been made—for example, the recent Batman movies—and I think audiences embrace them. This makes me wonder if the real culprit isn't the lowbrow tastes of the American audience, but the lowbrow talents of Hollywood screenwriters.
Argue	*Transformers* represents modern Hollywood in all its loud, stupid glory—two hours of visual noise more interested in blowing things up than ever really coming together as a coherent film.

---

3. A sample thesis might be the following: *Transformers* is an example of Hollywood at its worst—a clichéd plot plus bad acting, aimed only at making money and not challenging its viewers or advancing the action movie genre.

Lesson 6

Practice 1

Here is a sample chronological outline for the freewriting exercise in Lesson 3.

1. Studied all week to get ready for exam.
2. Taking exam—seeing everyone cheating. Very angry.
3. Typing up note at home.
4. Leaving note on teacher's desk.
5. Teacher confronting class.
6. People deciding it was Pearl who told on them.
7. Being mean to Pearl.
9. Feeling guilty.
10. Telling Rob.
11. Walking into cafeteria and having people make fun of me.
12. People avoiding me for weeks.

Practice 2

Here's an outline using order of importance for the school uniforms issue:

School uniforms: a good idea

A. Students and parents will save time and money.

   1. spend less time worrying about what to wear

   2. spend less time shopping

   3. spend less money on clothes (fewer clothes needed)

B. Students will be more confident.

   1. will equalize students who can afford the most stylish, expensive clothes with those who can't

   2. will take the focus away from appearance so students can focus more on schoolwork

     a. with more focus on work, students will do better in school

   3. will help students feel like they belong

     a. students need to feel like they belong to feel good about themselves

     b. uniforms create a sense of community and belonging

C. Students will be better disciplined.

   1. uniforms create a tone of seriousness

   2. uniforms make it easier to focus on schoolwork

Lesson 7

Practice 1

1. My topic will be how adolescence is represented in film. My goal is to show how and why the teenager is consistently characterized as an outsider who must seek to define him or herself apart from the crowd.

2. Looping #1: One thing I've always noticed about films with a teenage lead, or that are in a high school setting, is that the film is generally most interested in those characters who do not fit in or are not easily categorized into a typical social clique; lately, that character tends to be sarcastic, self-conscious, and different. These characters tend to be almost omnipotently aware of social behaviors and exceptionally bright (if not always mature); I sometimes wonder if they make high school look more fun than challenging. The more I think about it the more I recognize that it's very much an adult, not a teenage, vision of high school, and the ones writing it are those people who ended up writing and/or directing movies—the outsiders!

   Looping #2: The vision of high school we most commonly see on screen is the one crafted by those still coming to terms with their time there. In that sense, it's no wonder why high school is so alluring to Hollywood screenwriters: it's a chance to do it all over again, do and say the things they wish they had done when they were 17. At the same time, adults also want to imagine they were cooler and more original than they probably were, so it's no surprise that so many screen teens are wiser and trendier beyond their years and capable of an effortless cool no high school kid I know possesses.

3. My goal with this essay is to **show how and why the teenager is consistently characterized as an outsider who must seek to define him or herself apart from the crowd.** My own view is **that such a character type stems from the personalities of the writer or director involved in making the film** because **they ultimate determine the vision of adolescence, not actual teens, and it is highly likely that their adolescence was not satisfying and continues to linger on their mind.** Though I concede that **the outsider or anti-hero is a trait of hundreds of years of art and storytelling, I still maintain that it's especially true of mainstream contemporary films centered on adolescence, which have a distinctive predilection for shaggy-haired white males from the suburbs.** Although some might object that **such characterization is not the result of authorial bias but of metaphorical or biological intent,** I reply that **only a very narrow vision of teenage life is represented on-screen, and that is largely because a very singular kind of person is producing it.** The issue is important because **it helps clarify the perceptions and representation of youth in popular culture, as well as raises questions about the authenticity of recent portrayals of adolescent issues.**

Lesson 8

Practice 2

The following is the most logical way to divide the text into paragraphs (although minor variations are acceptable). Notice that each of the three parts of the personality gets its own paragraph. The topic sentence in each of those paragraphs (underlined) describes the main characteristic of that part of the personality.

Sigmund Freud, the father of psychoanalysis, made many contributions to the science of psychology. One of his greatest contributions was his theory of personality. <u>According to Freud, the human personality is made up of three parts: the id, the ego, and the superego.</u>

<u>The id is the part of the personality that exists only in the subconscious.</u> According to Freud, the id has no direct contact with the reality. It is the innermost core of our personality and operates according to the pleasure principle. That is, it seeks immediate gratification for its desires, regardless of external realities or consequences. It is not even aware that external realities or consequences exist.

<u>The ego develops from the id and is the part of the personality in contact with the real world.</u> The ego is conscious and therefore aims to satisfy the subconscious desire of the id as best it can without the individual's environment. When it can't satisfy those desires, it tried to control or suppress the id. The ego functions according to the reality principle.

The superego is the third and final part of the personality to develop. <u>This part of the personality contains our moral values and ideals, our notion of what's right and wrong.</u> The superego gives us the "rules" that help the ego control the id. For example, a child wants a toy that belongs to another child (id). He checks his environment to see if it's possible to take that toy (ego). He can, and does. But then he remembers that it's wrong to take something that belongs to someone else (superego) and returns the toy.

Lesson 9

Practice 1 and 2
Look again at the outline for school uniforms (a response for Practice 1 of Lesson 7), noticing how each of the three main supporting ideas has several supporting ideas of its own. In the following, you'll find additional support for one of those ideas. Notice the mix of specific examples, facts, reasons, descriptions, and expert opinion.

- Students will be more confident.
  - will equalize students who can afford the most stylish, expensive clothes with those who can't
  - students often judge each other based on dress
- The most popular kids are usually the ones who can also keep up with the most recent fashion trends. "In any school yard, all you have to do is look around to see how important clothing is in defining groups and determining social status. The most popular students are always the ones in the designer clothes. The least popular are often dressed in clothes that are two, three, or more fashion cycles out of date." Edward Jones, "The Clothes Make the Kid," <u>American View</u> magazine.
- Status is often determined by how you dress, not who you are.
  - A shirt that has an alligator or polo pony isn't just a shirt—it's a status symbol
  - "A student who wears 'retro' clothing will often be seen as 'cool' or 'hip,' while someone who wears polyester trousers and a pocket protector will be stereotyped as a 'nerd' or 'dork'—even though he may be just as 'hip' as she." Jamie Ernstein, professor of Cultural Studies, personal interview.
- Logos and labels have now become part of the design in clothing. A T-shirt that used to have a picture or geometric design will now sport the company's logo.
- If everyone has to wear uniforms, the social divisions created by those who can afford designer clothing and those who can't will disappear.
- Students will be judged for who they are, not for what they wear.

Lesson 10

Practice 2
Answers will vary, but must contain all four elements.

1. Thesis: Despite the dangers, the Internet should remain a totally free and uncensored medium.
2. Supporting Points:
   - Censorship would violate the right to free speech.
   - Censorship of material on the Internet could set a precedent for censorship of other media.
   - The courts would be clogged with cases regarding censorship because the definition of whatever material should be censored would necessarily be vague and subject to interpretation.
3. The Opposition's Position:
   - Hate speech, when it incites violence, does not fall under protection of the First Amendment.

- Nudity, cursing, and violence are limited on television, which kids can access 24 hours a day. How is the Internet different? Kids can access it 24 hours a day, too, with potentially no one around to control which sites they visit.
- Determining what kind of material should be censored will lead to a nationwide examination of our values.

4. Paragraph Acknowledging the Opposition:

Most importantly, censorship on the Internet violates one of the principles upon which this country was founded: freedom of speech. It is true that some sites present lewd or hateful images and ideas, but this kind of hate speech can be found anywhere, in all kinds of publications and all kinds of media. The Internet just makes it easier for people to find this information. If someone really wants to commit an act of violence, a website isn't what going to push him or her into committing a hate crime.

Lesson 11

Practice 1

This example uses surprising facts to catch the reader's attention:

At Jamestown Senior High, an amazing thing happened. In just one year, student thefts dropped from 58 to 18, assaults plunged from 32 to 5, and total disciplinary action plummeted from 112 to 42. The dramatic change at Jamestown High was created by the institution of a simple policy, one that should be instituted at middle and high schools nationwide: school uniforms.

Practice 2

In this introduction, an anecdote is used:

Paula always wore the same two or three outfits. She decided she'd rather be made fun of for wearing the same clothes all the time than for wearing the cheap, no-name gear that made up most of her wardrobe. At least these outfits gave her a shot at hanging out with the cool kids. At least she could proudly display the brand-name logos.

Unfortunately, Paula's attitude toward clothing is all too common among students who spend more time worrying about what they (and others) are wearing than about what they're supposed to be learning. School uniforms can help change that—and help fix a number of other problems that are plaguing our schools.

Lesson 12

Practice 1 and 2
Following are two possible conclusions for the school uniforms essay.
Closing with a question:

Of course, school uniforms won't solve every problem. Low-income kids will still be poor, violent students may still be violent, and advertisements will still assail us with the message that you can get what you want (the right guy, the right girl, the right friends, the right job) by buying and wearing trendy clothes. But school uniforms can help equalize the incredible division between the fashion "haves" and the "have nots"; they can improve discipline, and they can improve learning. In the same year the disciplinary incidents went down at Jamestown High, SAT scores went up. Wouldn't you like your school to do the same?

Closing with a call to action:

School uniforms aren't a cure-all, but in all of the public schools where school uniforms are now required, attendance and test scores are up, and disciplinary incidents are down. Students attest to feeling as if they're part of a community, and most say they like not having to worry about what to wear. More importantly, most say they actually feel better about themselves and school than they ever did before.

The power to create this kind of positive change is in your hands. Talk to your PTA and school board representatives. Show them the facts. Start a campaign to make school uniforms part of your child's education. You'll be glad you did—and so will they.

Lesson 13

Practice 1
Following is an additional supporting paragraph. Notice how its first sentence uses the word *example*.

Here's another example. Imagine you're at a diner. When the server hands you your check, you notice that she made a mistake, charging you $12.58 instead of $15.58. But you don't tell her. Instead, you pay $12.58 and pocket the $3.00 difference.

Practice 2
The following example revises and expands one of the paragraphs in the *lying with silence* essay:

Original:

I'm guilty, too. I knew my friend's boyfriend was also seeing someone else. But I kept quiet. I helped keep her in the dark. Then, when she found him out—and found out that I'd known about it—it was terrible. It destroyed their relationship and our friendship.

Revised and expanded:

I'm guilty of silent deceptions, too. For example, last year, I discovered that my friend Amy's boyfriend, Scott, was also seeing someone else. But I kept quiet about it because I didn't want to hurt Amy. A few weeks later, someone else told her about Scott's two-timing—and told her that I knew about it.

Amy couldn't believe I deceived her like that. She felt just as betrayed as if I'd lied to her face about it. Scott's deception ruined their relationship. My deception ruined our friendship.

Lesson 14

Practice 1

Your table should look something like this:

PARAGRAPH	IDEA	FUNCTION
3	when silence is a lie	addressing possible counterargument (that being silent isn't lying)
4	man who buys a necklace he knows is stolen	offers example of lie
5	consequences of his lie	offers evidence that silent lie is devastating
6	lying to Amy about Scott and consequences of that lie	offers another example and evidence of consequences
7	lying at diner	offers another example of silent lie
8	silent lies can be devastating; prosecute people who tell silent lies, not just "regular" lies	concludes essay

1. The essay is organized by order of importance, from most important to least important.
2. Probably not. For arguments, the best strategy is typically least to most important.
3. Reverse the order of the examples. Start with the diner scenario. Keep the Amy/Scott example second, and then end with the most powerful example—the man who knowingly bought a stolen necklace and gave it to his girlfriend.

Practice 2

Here's one way to revise the conclusion:

Silence can not only be deceitful—it can also be deadly. Before you decide to deceive someone with silence, consider the consequences of your action, and recognize it for what it is: a lie.

Lesson 15

Practice 1

Individual revisions will vary, but you should have addressed the following problems in the paragraph.

1st sentence:	unnecessary repetition and wordiness
2nd sentence:	unnecessary repetition and wordiness, passive sentence
3rd sentence:	pretentious language and wordiness
4th sentence:	passive sentence
5th sentence:	unnecessary repetition and ambiguity (does *they* refer to questions or opportunities?)

Here's how the edited paragraph might look:

The greatest challenge my generation will face will be ethical dilemmas created by scientific advances. We have discovered so much in this century, especially in the last few decades. We have opportunities to do things we never thought possible before. But these opportunities have raised some very difficult ethical questions. These opportunities have given us new power over nature, but this power can easily be abused.

Practice 2

The following is an example of a successful edit.

My generation will face many problems. First is the problem of feeling overwhelmed by technology. Second, with the ever-increasing life span of human beings, the generation gap is widening. A third problem is the population explosion; there are more people on the planet than ever before, and the world population continues to grow exponentially, putting a squeeze on our habitable space. That leads us to a fourth problem: limited natural resources.

Lesson 16

Practice 1

Here is the paragraph with run-ons, fragments, agreement errors, and confusing words corrected:

Comic relief is important in tragedies. Readers need a little relief from all of the sadness in the story. For example, consider Hamlet. After Ophelia dies, the next scene is with the gravedigger, who is a very funny character. He digs up a skull and makes a long speech about who the skull might have belonged to. Even though it is about death, the scene is funny, and it allows readers to forget about the tragedy for a moment and laugh.

Practice 2

Here is the paragraph with capitalization, punctuation, and spelling errors corrected:

Compact discs (CDs), which may be found in over 25 million American homes, not to mention backpacks and automobiles, first entered popular culture in the 1980s. But their history goes back to the 1960s, when an inventor named James Russell decided to create an alternative to his scratched and warped phonograph records—a system that could record, store, and replay music without ever wearing out.

Lesson 17

Practice

Each response will vary. Here's one that successfully fulfills the assignment:

Thesis: One of today's unsung heroes is my friend Mani Kaur.
Outline:

1. How I met Mani
   - behind her in line at the store
   - she was buying diapers
   - couldn't believe how many she was buying
   - I asked if she needed help carrying them to her car
   - found out she had just adopted three baby girls from China

2. Meeting the babies
   - told Mani I loved children
   - she invited me to come over and help out
   - went the next day
   - saw how great she was with the babies
   - saw how ill two of them looked

3. Why she adopted
   • told me about the law of having only one child
   • Mani and her husband couldn't have children of their own
   • wanted to rescue as many as they could, give them a better life

4. How can she handle it?
   • Mani's job—low paying (librarian), but flexible hours and close by
   • husband's job as marketing representative pays better, but he must travel three weeks each month
   • close network of family and friends to help out

5. Why is she a hero?
   • forever changing lives of three children
   • giving them a chance to grow up in a safe, loving home
   • setting an example for others, like me
   • a year later, babies all healthy, happy, well adjusted

Conclusion: Now when Mani goes to buy diapers, she always has someone to help—me.

Lessons 18 and 19

Practice
To estimate a grade for your timed essay, look at the scoring chart on pages 174–175. Read your essay and evaluate it by using this scoring system. After you assign a number for each of the categories shown on the scoring chart, average the numbers to get an overall score. A 5 is an "A," a 4 is a "B," and so on.

Posttest, Part 1

If you miss any of the answers, you can find help for that question type in the lesson(s) shown to the right of the answer.

QUESTION	ANSWER	LESSON
1.	b.	1, 2
2.	d.	1
3.	c.	12
4.	a.	9
5.	d.	6, 7
6.	b.	10
7.	d.	9, 15
8.	a.	2
9.	c.	14–17
10.	b.	16
11.	a.	13
12.	a.	6, 7
13.	c.	17
14.	b.	18
15.	b.	12
16.	d.	16
17.	e.	5, 8
18.	b.	5, 6
19.	d.	15
20.	a.	11

Posttest, Part 2

Use the scoring chart on pages 174–175 to evaluate your essay. After you assign a number for each of the categories shown on the chart, average the numbers to get an overall score.

ADDITIONAL RESOURCES ▶

Grammar and Mechanics

Websites

www.grammarbook.com: the popular Blue Book of Grammar and Punctuation online, with simple explanations of grammar and punctuation pitfalls, and separate exercises and answer keys

www.m-w.com: Merriam-Webster Online. This site has a number of interesting features that will make you forget you are trying to improve your spelling!

www.protrainco.com/info/grammar.htm: The Professional Training Company's "Good Grammar, Good Style pages"

www.spelling.hemscott.net: Useful advice on how to improve your spelling

www.wsu.edu/~brians/errors/index.html: Paul Brians's "Common Errors in English"

Books

Practical Spelling, 2nd Edition. (LearningExpress, 2007).

Fowler, H.W., revised by Robert W. Burchfield, *The New Fowler's Modern English Usage*, revised 3rd Edition (Oxford University Press, 2008)

Johnson, Edward D., *The Handbook of Good English* (Washington Square Press, 1991)

LearningExpress, *1001 Vocabulary and Spelling Questions: Fast, Focused Practice to Help You Improve Your Word Skills* (LearningExpress, 1999)

LearningExpress, *Grammar Essentials, 3rd Edition* (LearningExpress, 2006)

Merriam-Webster, *Merriam-Webster's Guide to Punctuation and Style* (Merriam-Webster, 2002)

O'Conner, Patricia T., *Woe Is I: The Grammarphobe's Guide to Better English in Plain English*, 3rd Edition (Riverhead Trade, 2009)

Princeton Review, *Grammar Smart: A Guide to Perfect Usage*, 2nd Edition (Princeton Review, 2001)

Strunk, William, and E.B. White, *The Elements of Style*, 4th Edition (Longman, 2000)

Essay Exam Information

- **ACT**

    Online information, study tips, and practice test: www.actstudent.org.

    Books: The creator of the ACT published *The Real ACT Prep Guide with CD, 3rd Edition* in 2011 (Peterson's Guides).

- **SAT**

    Online information from the creator of the SAT: www.collegeboard.com.

    Books: Since the SAT essay was given for the first time in 2005, be certain you use only the latest editions of SAT preparation and information books. Good ones include *The Official SAT Study Guide, 2nd Edition*, and *10 Real SATs*, both published by The College Board.

- **GED**

    www.philaliteracy.org is the Mayor of Philadelphia's Commission on Literacy's site, with information on how to prepare for the GED essay. For more information about the GED, go to www.gedtest.org.

    Books: Check out LearningExpress's *Acing the GED*.

- **Regents'**

    www.usg.edu is the state of Georgia Regents' Site, with sample essay test forms, list of topics, and scoring information. Search for specific information on your state's test using your state name and "Regent's essay" as search terms.

Supplemental Writing Prompts

501 Writing Prompts (LearningExpress, 2007)

www.4tests.com has free practice tests modeled on the ACT, GED, and SAT essay sections, plus links to many good test-preparation sites.

Online Writing Resources

www.bartleby.com
Without a doubt, the best online reference site on the Web. It has a searchable database of reference guides, encyclopedias, and much more. Just some of the works you'll find here include *The American Heritage Dictionary of the English Language*, *Fowler's Modern English Usage*, *The Elements of Style*, and *The American Heritage Book of English Usage*.

grammar.ccc.commntet.edu/grammar
This guide to grammar and writing, maintained by Professor Charles Darling of Capital Community College, Hartford, CT, is a comprehensive site with a particularly useful "ask grammar" service.

www.askoxford.com
This site has sections on classic errors and helpful hints, better writing, and ask the experts. You can sign up for "word of the day" e-mails and chat with others about language questions.

Suggestions for Great Writing

- *Harper's* (weekly magazine)
- *The Atlantic* (monthly magazine)
- *The Economist* (London-based weekly magazine; check it out online at www.economist.com)
- *The New Yorker* (weekly magazine)
- *The Best American Essays 2011*, Edwidge Danticat, editor (Mariner Books, 2011)
- *One Hundred Great Essays 4th Edition*, Robert DiYanni (Longman, 2010)
- *The Best American Science Writing 2011*, Rebecca Skloot and Floyd Skloot, editors (Harper Collins, 2011).

ADDITIONAL ONLINE PRACTICE ▶

Whether you need help building basic skills or preparing for an exam, visit the LearningExpress Practice Center! On this site, you can access additional practice materials. Using the code below, you'll be able to get free essay writing practice online.

Log in to the LearningExpress Practice Center by using this URL: **www.learnatest.com/practice**

This is your access code: **7922**

Follow the steps online to redeem your access code. After you've used your access code to register with the site, you will be prompted to create a username and password. For easy reference, record them here:

Username: _____ **Password:** _____

With your username and password, you can log in and access your additional practice material. If you have any questions or problems, please contact LearningExpress customer service at 1-800-295-9556 ext. 2, or e-mail us at **customerservice@learningexpressllc.com**.